10 0299550 8

KU-475-097

DOROTHY JONGEWARD
MURIEL JAMES
Human Relations and Communications Consultants

WINNING WITH PEOPLE

Group Exercises in Transactional Analysis

ADDISON-WESLEY PUBLISHING COMPANY

Reading, Massachusetts   Menlo Park, California   New York
Don Mills, Ontario   Wokingham, England   Amsterdam   Bonn
Sydney   Singapore   Tokyo   Madrid   San Juan   Paris
Seoul   Milan   Mexico City   Taipei

Illustrations by Ned Williams

Copyright © 1973 by Addison-Wesley Publishing Company, Inc.

All rights reserved. No part of this publication may be reproduced, stored
in a retrieval system, or transmitted, in any form or by any means,
electronic, mechanical, photocopying, recording, or otherwise, without the
prior written permission of the publisher. Printed in the United States of
America. Published simultaneously in Canada.

ISBN 0-201-03314-3
26 27 28 29 30 - AL - 94939291
Twenty-sixth printing, July 1991

100299 550 8

INTRODUCTION

People are interested in learning new ideas fast. Workbooks can accelerate this process. This workbook is, in part, an adaptation from our book <u>Born to Win: Transactional Analysis With Gestalt Experiments</u>.* It is designed as a group-oriented training tool for rapid learning of transactional analysis principles. It can be used in conjunction with <u>Born to Win</u> as a text or it can be used alone.

Currently we find a resurgence of interest in the "why" and "how" of human behavior and in man's search for meaning in his existence. Bosses study how to work with subordinates; parents take courses on rearing children; husbands and wives learn to talk to each other and how to "fight fair", and teachers study how to cope with emotional disturbances in their students and how to reverse the effects of deprivation.

Along with their interest in material goods and technology, many people are concerning themselves with what it means to be human. As one young male executive in a large firm put it, "I have a Master's degree in accounting. When I went to work with this firm, I thought my problems were going to be accounting problems, But they're not. They're 'people' problems."

Our new approach to understanding people is transactional analysis as developed by Dr. Eric Berne. According to Dr. Berne, his theories evolved as he observed behavioral changes occurring in a patient when a new stimulus, such as a word, gesture, or sound, entered his focus. These changes involved facial expressions, word intonations, sentence structure, body movements, gestures, tics, posture, and carriage. It was as though there were several different people inside the individual. At times one or the other of these inner different people seemed to be in control of the patient's total personality.

He observed that these various "selves" transacted with other people in different ways and that these transactions could be analyzed. He saw that some of the transactions had ulterior motives; the individual used them as a means of manipulating others into psychological games and rackets.† He also observed that people performed in predetermined ways — acting as if they were on stage and reading from a theatrical script. These observations led Berne to develop his unique theory called Transactional Analysis, abbreviated to TA.

Originally TA was developed as a method of psychotherapy to be used in group treatment. The group serves as a setting in which people can become more aware of themselves, the structure of their individual personality, how they transact with others, the games they play, and the scripts they act out.

---

* Reading, Massachusetts: Addison-Wesley, 1971.

† The analysis of games has received wide popularity in Berne's bestseller, <u>Games People Play</u>.

Such awareness enables persons to see themselves more clearly so that they can change what they want to change and strengthen what they want to strengthen.

TA is not only a useful tool for those in psychotherapy: it also provides a thought-provoking perspective of human behavior that most people can understand and put to use. It encourages the use of words that are simple, direct, and often colloquial, instead of psychological, scientific words or jargon. For example, the major parts of the personality are called <u>Parent</u>, <u>Adult</u>, and <u>Child</u>.

Transactional analysis is a rational approach to understanding behavior and is based on the assumption that people can learn to trust themselves, think for themselves, make their own decisions, and express their feelings. Its principles can be applied on the job, in the home, in the classroom, in the neighborhood — wherever people deal with people.

10029995508

We designed this workbook for a seminar that lasts several days. You may wish to cover the basic principles of transactional analysis in a shorter period. If so, we suggest that you use only those sections which are most relevant to your organization and which help you reach the behavioral objectives you have set for your group. (See Appendix A on page 113 for suggestions.)

When you have established your goals, check through all the units in the workbook and include in your course only those units most necessary to reach your goals in the time allowed. While this workbook can be used cover to cover, it is also designed so that a few units can be used if time is short or if only selected TA concepts are pertinent.

For example, if you have only a day or a day and a half, and are a group leader in a class where the principles of TA are to be applied to customer-contact problems, the most useful concepts to cover are ego states, transactions, stamps, and perhaps games. For this type of training experience, have the participants work through Units 2, 3, 4, and 5. You may discover that there are more exercises than you need or have time for. Select the most relevant. On the other hand, in a university course aimed at teaching the theory of TA, there would be time to work through most of the workbook even though all the exercises might not be used.

We believe that group participants learn from each other. Therefore, whenever possible and practical we hope you will give the participants time to work together on the exercises in small groups of five or six. Much of the learning can be their responsibility. We also suggest that, if practical, each group give a brief report of its decisions and experiences to the overall group.

A few of the exercises, such as the very personal questions about script, can be done individually. However, depending on the goals and purpose of the seminar, even these may be useful to share in small groups and/or in a general class discussion. One team, working with delinquent boys, found it useful to discuss openly their own early life messages, personality structure, and transactional patterns so that they could develop a better working relationship within their team and a better understanding of their relationship with their charges.

A transactional analysis bibliography, reference to other materials, and the address of the International Transactional Analysis Association (ITAA) are included in Appendix B (page 115).

The aims of our workbook are (1) to give you an introduction to the major concepts of transactional analysis, and (2) to allow you, through the exercises and group participation, to discover and validate as much as possible from your own insights and experiences and from those of others.

CONTENTS

Contents   viii

Contents   x

UNIT 1. THE SCRIPTS PEOPLE LIVE BY

Do you know anyone who is successful in his personal life and on the job and also well liked?

Do you know anyone who is a plodder who works and works and doesn't get very far?

Do you know anyone who shows up at work but feels futile about his job and is really waiting for retirement?

Do you know anyone who always performs in the same failure-oriented way and inevitably is criticized or even rejected?

Do you know anyone who says he wishes he'd never been born?

If you do, then you know what it's like watching someone act out a psychological script.

PEOPLE LIVE BY SCRIPTS

In the life of every individual the dramatic life events, the roles that are learned, rehearsed, and acted out, are originally determined by a script - a life drama a person may be unaware of but feels compelled to live by.

People play out their scripts within the context of the society in which they live and which have their own dramatic patterns. As Shakespeare said, all the world is a stage. Cultures follow scripts; families follow scripts; individuals follow scripts. Each individual's life is a unique drama which can include elements of both family and cultural scripts. The interplay of these scripts affects the drama of each person's life, and thereby unfolds the history of a people.

CULTURES HAVE SCRIPTS

Cultural scripts are the accepted and expected dramatic patterns that occur within a society. They are determined by the spoken and unspoken assumptions believed by the majority of people within that group about expected roles, stage directions, costumes, settings, and final curtains. Cultural scripts reflect what is thought of as the "national character," and the same drama may be repeated generation after generation.

Cultural scripts usually dictate specific roles. Most cultures differentiate—rationally or irrationally—between the roles men are to play and the roles expected of women. Most cultures have favorite postures and gestures centered around such things as rituals, sexual behaviors, and manners.

Some individuals accept their cultural script, some do not. If an individual's life drama fits the expectations of his or her culture, acceptance and approval are received. For example, if "making money" is the cultural focus, those who do well financially are highly regarded. Their individual scripts are harmonious with that of their culture.

Others in the same culture may be considered failures if they choose to pursue their own interests, ideas, or talents and reject the "making money" theme. Because their personal scripts are out of harmony with that of their culture, they are likely to receive disapproval, ridicule, or punishment from others. When cultural scripts are perpetuated, it is usually done so through the family. Many families have traditional expectations for the life goals, roles, social status, and so forth of the family members.

PEOPLE HAVE INDIVIDUAL PSYCHOLOGICAL SCRIPTS

Whenever people get together in groups there are likely to be those who try to play it cool, or play it straight, or play at being the intellectual, or play like a birdbrain. They often choose their clothes, fix their hair, wear makeup, and so on to fit the role they play.

In addition they choose friends, spouses, and fellow-workers, expecting them to play complementary parts in a preprogrammed life drama. The slave looks for the master; the nurse looks for the invalid; the criminal looks for the judge.

In the life of every individual the dramatic events and the roles that are learned, rehearsed, and acted out are originally determined by a psychological script. Most people, often without knowing it, design their behavior, their facial expressions, even their words as though they were "on stage" either as a main character or in a supporting role. Indeed, all the world is a stage and each person plays the parts his or her script calls for.

A particular script may call for a superman (or woman), a serious plodder, a tragic clown. It may, for example, call for excitement and achievement, for boredom and passivity, or for depression and failure. For better or worse, whatever the script calls for is likely to be acted out, unless a person consciously decides otherwise.

A psychological script bears a striking resemblance to a theatrical script. Each has a prescribed cast of characters, dialogue, acts and scenes, themes and plots, which move toward a climax and end with a final curtain. A psychological script is a person's ongoing program for his or her life drama which dictates where he or she is going in life and how to get there. It is a drama compulsively acted out, though one's awareness of it may be vague.

Within any drama there are usually the basic roles of Persecutor, Rescuer, and Victim. [1] † These roles interchange constantly. For example, someone who acts like a Victim usually ends up persecuting others, making them feel guilty, i.e., "You never take me out to dinner." Someone who chooses the roles of Persecutor may be punishing one person while rescuing another, i.e., "I'll give you a beating if you don't leave your Mother alone." Someone who acts like a Rescuer often persecutes others by keeping them overly dependent, i.e. "Now, don't you worry. I'll see that the job is finished right."

Life dramas have varying degrees of constructiveness, destructiveness, or nonproductiveness — going nowhere. Each has a unique set of expectations and calls for unique scenery, dialogue, and characters. Each reflects the cultural and family traditions of the past. Each has elements of winning †† and/or losing.

---

† Numbers in brackets refer to footnotes and references for each chapter which begins on page 111.
†† Your authors describe winners as actualizing persons — people who are responding to life authentically and most fully being themselves. [2]

Scripts can be recognized in daily life. Most people experience, and also observe others, acting compulsively in certain ways, living up to specific identities, and fulfilling a sense of destiny.

SCRIPTING STARTS NONVERBALLY

Psychological scripts are selected in childhood. They often resemble a favorite childhood story which is "rewritten" and rehearsed in a more sophisticated version in adolescence. The show goes on the road when a person enters his early twenties.

In the life of any one individual, the most important forces in forming the script are the "messages," including instructions, sent by parent figures. Some children are wanted, some are not. At birth they may be accepted or rejected because of sex, appearance, color, size, and so forth. Even the circumstances of birth—pain, cost, convenience, family relationships, attitudes of relatives (including in-laws)—may affect the dramatic attitudes and actions parents take toward their children.

An infant, almost as if he had radar, begins to pick up verbal and nonverbal messages about himself and his worth through his first experiences of being touched or being ignored by others. An infant who is cuddled affectionately, smiled at, and talked to receives messages that are likely to contribute to a constructive life drama. An infant who is handled with fright, hostility, or anxiety is likely to get messages that lead to nonproductive (going nowhere) or destructive life dramas. Basic to anyone's script is the self-image taken on in infancy.

This self-image may be affected by a child's name. Names often imply the roles parents expect children to play. These roles are frequently tied to a particular person the child is expected to copy—a grandparent, a favorite aunt or uncle, a tragic clown, a biblical character, a national hero, or a well-known movie star.

SCRIPT MESSAGES ARE ALSO VERBALIZED

As an infant grows into childhood, he or she begins to understand the scripting messages that parents put into words. "You're so wonderful." "See, isn't he/she amazing!"

In response to the words "You'll be famous someday," a person may find a way to get on the cover of a magazine—perhaps through a career, perhaps by building something, writing something, or creating something, perhaps by taking a stand or achieving the unusual.

In response to the words "You'll never amount to anything," a person may fail in school, get a poorly paid job, be unable to find a loving spouse, be a poor parent, and/or just "never quite make it." Whether negative or positive, people tend to follow their parents' instructions and fulfill their expectations.

As children grow older, parents script them in specific areas of their lives. They tell them what to hope for and what to fear in marriage and family life. They tell them what kind and how much education to get, even where to get it. They encourage health or illness, acceptable or unacceptable behavior.

Parents can even script children vocationally if they frequently make statements such as:

"George was cut out to be a doctor."
"You'd make a great teacher."
"You could sell refrigerators to Eskimos."
"What a nurse you'd make!"
"With your gift of gab, you could be a lawyer."

Script messages are like stage directions that a person later feels compelled to follow as a part of his life drama. The directions may be positive and/or negative, verbal or nonverbal, consistent or inconsistent. In response to them children make decisions to comply or to rebel.

Note to leader: The purpose of the exercises on scripts is not to do an in-depth personal survey but to begin to understand how scripts are formed and how scripts are acted out.

EXERCISE 1. PARENTAL SCRIPT MESSAGES

What messages might parents say about:

doing work _____   using money _____

_____   _____

_____   _____

getting educated _____   being a man _____

_____   _____

_____   _____

being religious _____   being a woman _____

_____   _____

_____   _____

achieving success _____   being good or bad _____

_____   _____

_____   _____

having brains _____   developing talents _____

_____   _____

_____   _____

being good looking or ugly ___

_____

_____

being graceful or clumsy_____

_____

_____

enjoying your body_____

_____

being an achiever or a non-

achiever_____

_____

_____

SCRIPTS ARE RELATED TO LIFE POSITIONS

Everyone was once a child and everyone develops a concept about individual worth by the age of six. Everyone also formulates ideas about the worth of others. This is done by crystallizing individual experiences and making decisions about what life means, what parts will be played, and how the parts of the life script will be acted out. These are the days of decision [3]— the time when one makes a commitment to acting in certain ways which become part of one's character. Decisions made very early in life about self and others may be quite unrealistic, although they seem logical and make sense to a child at the time he makes them.

For example, if children are ridiculed and frequently called stupid, they can decide by the time they are four years old that they are stupid and other people know it all. They will begin to develop their role and to act that way. They base their life script on the position "I'm not-OK" but "You (meaning other people) are OK." When they go to school, they may fail, feeling they can't do anything right and lack brains.

As they grow older, they will further fulfill their own prophecy by acting out their psychological positions on their jobs and in their personal lives. They often make mistakes for which they are reprimanded. Thus they feel stupid, again maintaining their own status-quo.

Any person's script will be related to three basic questions: Who am I? What am I doing here? Who are all those other people? [4]

Decisions are the basis for life positions. These positions, even if negative, are crystallized, often subconsciously, into script roles. For example, a person who has a gut-level feeling of I'm not-OK and You're OK may say to a co-worker, or a spouse or a friend, "Gee, you seem to be able to do everything right the first time. Look at me. I still can't do it well," or (whining), "Why do things like this always happen to me? You never seem to have this kind of trouble," or, "I'm so stupid! How can you stand to put up with me?"

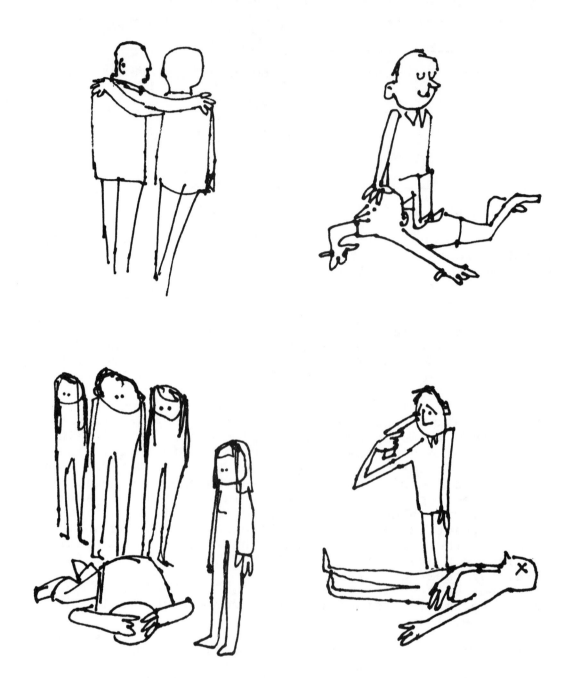

When taking positions about themselves, people may conclude:

>   I do many things right.
>   I do everything wrong.

>   I don't deserve to live.
>   I'm as good as anybody else.

>   I can't think for myself.
>   I have a good head on my shoulders.

When taking positions about others, a person may conclude:

>   People are wonderful.
>   People are no damn good.

>   People will help me.
>   People are out to get me.

>   People can't be trusted.
>   People are basically honest.

The above positions can be generalized: "I'm OK" or "I'm not-OK," are "You're OK" or "You're not-OK." They fit together to form the four basic life positions [5].

The First Position: I'm OK, You're OK

is potentially a mentally healthy position. If realistic, people with this position about themselves and others can solve their problems constructively. Their expectations are likely to be valid. They accept the significance of people.

The Second Position: I'm OK, You're not-OK

is the position of persons who feel victimized or persecuted. They blame others for their miseries. Delinquents and criminals often have this position and take on paranoid behavior which in extreme cases may lead to homicide.

The Third or Introjective Position: I'm not-OK, You're OK

is a common position of persons who feel powerless when they compare themselves to others. This position leads them to withdraw, to experience depression, and, in severe cases, to become suicidal.

The Fourth or Futility Position: I'm not-OK, You're not-OK

is the position of those who lose interest in living, who exhibit schizoid behavior, and, in extreme cases, commit suicide and/or homicide.

EXERCISE 2. LIFE POSITIONS AS A CHILD

Discuss in small groups how a child might take his life positions. Write below what kinds of experiences in his first eight years might lead him to decide:

I'm OK and You're OK _____

_____

_____

_____

_____

I'm OK and You're not-OK _____

_____

_____

_____

_____

I'm not-OK and You're OK _____

_____

_____

_____

_____

I'm not-OK and You're not-OK _____

_____

_____

_____

_____

EXERCISE 3. LIFE POSITIONS AND LATER BEHAVIOR

Discuss in small groups how a grown-up might act out his life positions taken in childhood.

I'm OK and You're OK _____

_____

_____

_____

_____

I'm OK and You're not-OK _____

_____

_____

_____

_____

I'm not-OK and You're OK _____

_____

_____

_____

_____

I'm not-OK and You're not-OK _____

_____

_____

_____

_____

Note to leader: This exercise can be lengthy. Select only those parts relevent to your group and suitable for the time. You may want to divide up parts.

EXERCISE 4. LIFE POSITIONS CHART

Consider each of the life positions in terms of how a person such as a manager, teacher, spouse, student, co-worker, etc. would behave.

	I'm not-OK You're OK	I'm OK You're not-OK	I'm not-OK You're not-OK	I'm OK You're OK
List three adjectives that describe this person.				
Role most frequently played (Victim, Rescuer, and/or Persecutor)				
Feelings most likely to have (depression, anger, guilt)				
Approach to handling conflict				
Ways of giving compliments				
Ways of receiving compliments				

Note to leader: The first part of this exercise is on individual fantasy experience. It can be followed by group discussion.

EXERCISE 5. CULTURAL AND FAMILY SCRIPTING

Imagine yourself moving back in time. What were your ancestors like 75 years ago or 150 years ago?

- Does your cultural heritage affect you in any way today (i.e., in your sexual roles, work, educational aspirations)?

- Think of at least one thing you do now that is culturally determined.

- Think of the dramatic patterns in the family you grew up in. Are you repeating any of them now? What have you changed?

Note to leader: Exercises 6 and 7 are personal. They may be used for homework if class discussion is inappropriate.

EXERCISE 6. YOUR OPINION OF YOURSELF

Were you told you were just like your father? mother? black-sheep uncle? brother? sister? or whom?

_____

_____

Were you compared to anyone? _____

If so, in what ways?

_____

_____

Say in a sentence what you imagine each of your parent figures thought of you when you were a child.

_____

_____

What do you think of yourself now?

_____

_____

Is your current self-appraisal related in any way to your parents' opinion of you as a child?

_____

_____

EXERCISE 7. YOUR LIFE DRAMA

Find a quiet place where you can sit down and not be interrupted. Close your eyes. Project your life drama on an imaginary screen in front of you. Watch it from its beginning up to the present moment. Take your time. After your experience, consider:

- Is it a comedy, a farce, a saga, a soap opera, a melodrama, a tragedy, or what?

- Does your play have a script theme? If so, is it success-oriented or failure-oriented? constructive, destructive, or nonproductive?

- Imagine the audience watching your play. Do they applaud, cry, boo, laugh, go to sleep, want their money back, or what?

- Now ask yourself, "Was I ever told how I would end up?"

- If so, are you living up to this expectation?

- How do you think people like yourself actually do end up?

SUMMARY

People base their script, their life drama that they feel
compelled to act out, on the decisions that they make about
themselves and others in childhood. These decisions lead to
the various positions that in turn lead to different kinds of
life dramas. These dramas are constructive, destructive, or
going nowhere. They are often depicted in a culture's
mythology, folklore, or fairy tales.
    Hearing or seeing these stories children may try to live
out a similar drama as their favorite character if the character
fits their position. Life dramas affect how people act in their
social and personal life and what they say and do on the job.
They may follow such patterns as always fumbling, never quite
making it, getting to the top, getting put down, getting
things their way, putting others down, losing the job, always
striving, working themselves to death, enjoying their life,
growing on the job, being themselves, etc.
    Transactional analysis (TA) can be used to break up a
negative script, to turn off destructive messages, to allow
a person to become even more autonomous and to make up an
individual life drama. It can help a person change what he
or she chooses to change.

UNIT 2. THE PERSONALITIES PEOPLE DEVELOP

Do you know anyone who points an accusing finger at others just as his father did?

Do you know anyone who works hard taking care of others just as her mother did?

Do you know anyone who collects facts, thinks things through, and acts rationally?

Do you know anyone who throws temper tantrums as he did at age 3?

Do you know anyone who learned as a child to "be seen but not heard"?

If so, you have seen the three ego states that make up personality in action— the Parent ego state, the Adult ego state, and the Child ego state. Together these three ego states form personality structure.

EVERYONE HAS THREE EGO STATES

Dr. Eric Berne (originator of the theory of transactional analysis and author of the popular book, <u>Games People Play</u>) defines an ego state as "a consistent pattern of feeling and experience directly related to a corresponding consistent pattern of behavior." [1]

The implications are that what happens to a person is recorded in the brain and nervous tissue. This includes everything a person experiences in childhood, all that is incorporated from parent figures, perceptions of events, the feelings associated with these events, and the distortions in one's memory. These recordings are stored as though on video tape. They can be replayed, and the event recalled and even reexperienced.

Each person has three ego states which are separate and distinct sources of behavior: The Parent ego state, the Adult ego state, and the Child ego state. These are not abstract concepts but realities. "Parent, Adult, and Child represent real people who now exist or who once existed, who have legal names and civic identities." [2]

The structure of personality is diagrammed as follows:

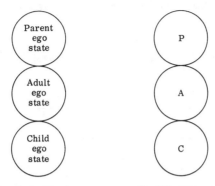

Ego State Structure   Simplified Diagram

Ego states are colloquially termed Parent, Adult, and
Child. When capitalized in this workbook they will refer to
ego states, not to actual parents, adults, or children.

The Parent ego state contains the attitudes and behavior
incorporated from external sources, primarily parents. Outwardly, it is often expressed toward others in prejudicial,
critical, and nurturing behavior. Inwardly, it is experienced
as old Parental messages which continue to influence the
inner Child.

The Adult ego state is not related to a person's age. It
is oriented to current reality and the objective gathering of
information. It is organized, adaptable, intelligent, and
functions by testing reality, estimating probabilities, and
computing dispassionately.

The Child ego state contains all the impulses that come
naturally to an infant. It also contains the recordings of
past early experiences, responses to them, and the "positions"
taken about self and others. It is expressed as "old"
(archaic) behavior from childhood.

When you are acting, thinking, feeling, as you observed
your parents to be doing, you are in your Parent ego state.

When you are dealing with current reality, gathering
facts, and computing objectively, you are in your Adult ego
state.

When you are feeling and acting as you did when you were
a child, you are in your Child ego state.

EXERCISE 1.   ANALYZING EGO STATE VOCABULARY AND BODY LANGUAGE

<u>Parent:</u> Develop a list of words or phrases that are representative of the Parent ego state (i.e., should, don't).

_____   _____   _____

_____   _____   _____

Develop a list of gestures, postures, tone of voice, facial expressions, etc., that are representative of Parent ego state nonverbal and/or extraverbal behavior.

_____   _____   _____

_____   _____   _____

<u>Adult:</u> Develop a list of words and phrases that are representative of the Adult ego state (i.e., probably, estimate).

_____   _____   _____

_____   _____   _____

Develop a list of postures, gestures, tone of voice, facial expressions, etc., that are representative of the Adult ego state.

_____   _____   _____

_____   _____   _____

<u>Child:</u> Develop a list of words or phrases that are representative of the Child ego state (i.e., wow, I wish).

_____   _____   _____

_____   _____   _____

Develop a list of postures, gestures, voice tones, facial expressions, etc., that are representative of the Child ego state.

_____   _____   _____

_____   _____   _____

Note to leader: A few suggested responses are noted by your authors in Appendix C. The participants may wish to turn to these after completing this exercise. However, any response that can be justified by a person's personal history is acceptable. Remember that it is often the way the words are delivered that determines the ego state.

EVERYONE HAS PARENT FIGURES PROGRAMMED

The Parent ego state is the incorporation of the attitudes and behavior of all emotionally significant people who serve as parent figures to the child. The Parent ego state does not necessarily function in ways culturally defined as "motherly" or "fatherly."

THE PARENT EGO STATE IS EXPRESSED OUTWARDLY

When a Parent ego state is expressed outwardly, people transact with the ego states of others as they observed their own parents doing.

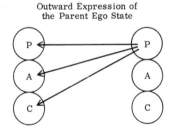

Outward Expression of
the Parent Ego State

For example, a meeting chairperson might tap a pencil on the table to make a point just as his or her parent might have done. Later a congratulatory pat would be given, again imitating his or her parent. At the same meeting a competent person who wants to speak up may sit silently, again imitating what his or her parent might do in front of a group of people.

THE PARENT EGO STATE IS EXPRESSED INWARDLY

People not only act toward others as their parents did, they also hear parental messages in their heads. These messages are similar to video tape recordings. They are experienced as an inner dialogue — Parent tapes heard by the Adult and especially the Child.

Inward Influence of
the Parent Ego State

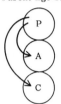

Some Parental messages are encouraging. Some are not. This inner dialogue may be permissive, confusing, supportive, condemning, moral, or rigidly moralistic.

For example, a person who is asked to present a point of view at a meeting may hear the old Parent tape, "Don't make a fool of yourself in front of other people." Another person asked a similar question may hear, "Don't be afraid to give it a try."

PARENTS EXHIBIT NURTURING AND PUNITIVE BEHAVIOR

Parents may be sympathetic, protective, and nurturing on some occasions and critical, prejudicial, moralizing, or punitive on others. Some parents tend to be more nurturing than judgmental, while others are more judgmental than nurturing.

A Child with nurturing parents develops an individual Parent ego state that contains nurturing behavior. With punitive parents a child is likely to be punitive at times.

The Parent ego state tends to be filled with opinions and prejudices about religion, politics, traditions, sexual role expectations, life styles, child rearing, proper dress, ways of speech, and so forth. A person acting from the critical side of the Parent ego state may come on as a bossy know-it-all whose behavior intimidates the Child in other people. A boss, spouse, teacher, or friend who frequently uses the critical Parent ego state may irritate other people and perhaps alienate them.

THERE ARE EGO STATES WITHIN THE PARENT

Each parent has three unique ego states in which the Parent, Adult, and Child ego state of parents, grandparents, older siblings, and babysitters have most likely been incorporated. At times parents behave toward their children as their parents behave toward them—moralizing, punishing, nurturing, ignoring. At other times parents reason on the basis of current objective data—explaining why, demonstrating how, searching for facts, and solving problems. At still other times they use behavior from their own childhood—whining, withdrawing, frolicking, giggling, manipulating, and playing. Therefore, when a person responds from the Parent ego state, what has been incorporated from any parent figure may affect the behavior that is demonstrated. The grandparents most often influence the Parent ego state of the parent.

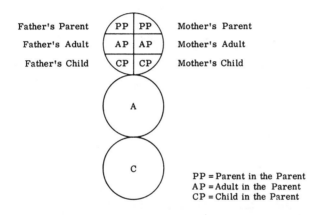

Father's Parent	PP	PP	Mother's Parent
Father's Adult	AP	AP	Mother's Adult
Father's Child	CP	CP	Mother's Child

A

C

PP = Parent in the Parent
AP = Adult in the Parent
CP = Child in the Parent

This means that at times a person's behavior may resemble grandmother's Adult or babysitter's Parent or father's Child, and so forth. The following story illustrates how certain traditions and beliefs — cultural and family scripts — may go back many generations, although the reasons behind them are long forgotten.

A bride served baked ham, and her husband asked why she cut the ends off. "Well, that's the way mother always did it," she replied. The next time his mother-in-law stopped by, he asked her why she cut the ends off the ham. "That's the way my mother did it," she replied.

And when grandma visited, she too was asked why she sliced the ends off. She said, "That's the only way I could get it into the pan."[3]

EXERCISE 2. GETTING TO KNOW YOUR PARENT EGO STATE

<u>Parent ego state</u>

a) Write three things that your parents did that you didn't like.

_____

_____

_____

b) Write three things that your parents did that you did like.

_____

_____

_____

c) Now study these lists and ask yourself, Do I do any of these things
myself? If so, with whom?

_____

_____

_____

d) Write down two important Parental messages that you still hear in
your head.

_____

_____

_____

e) Are these negative or positive? _____

f) Do they still influence your behavior in any way? Where? With whom?

_____

_____

_____

EXERCISE 3. RECOGNIZING NURTURING AND PUNITIVE PARENTAL
             BEHAVIOR

The Parent ego state often contains punitive or critical messages. Develop
three critical messages that you might hear at home, in your family, or in
your organization that sound like the Parent ego state.

_____

_____

_____

The Parent ego state often contains nurturing messages—protective, sympathetic, "taking-care-of" messages. Develop three nurturing Parent statements that you might hear in daily life.

_____

_____

_____

Think of three situations in which you were critical of other people.

_____

_____

_____

Was your behavior similar to the behavior of your parents? _____

Think of ways you nurture other people.

_____

_____

_____

Are these ways similar to the ways your parents nurtured you?

_____

EVERYONE HAS A CHILD EGO STATE

Within the brain and nervous system, everyone carries
permanent recordings of what has been experienced as a
child in terms of individual impulses, feelings about
the world, and adaptation to it.

　　When a person responds as he or she did in childhood —
inquisitive, affectionate, selfish, mean, playful, whining,
manipulative — he or she is responding from the Child ego
state.

　　The Child ego state develops into three discernable
parts: the Natural Child, the Little Professor, and the
Adapted Child. This is diagrammed as follows:

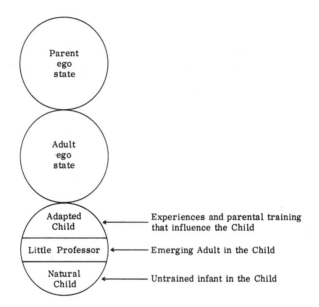

THE NATURAL CHILD IS UNCENSORED

The Natural Child is that part of the Child ego state that is the very young, impulsive, untrained, expressive infant still inside each person. It is often like a self-centered, pleasure-loving baby responding with cozy affection when needs are being met or with angry rebellion when they are not met.

The Natural Child within each person's Child ego state is what a baby would be "naturally" if no other influences were involved. The Natural Child is affectionate, impulsive, sensuous, uncensored, and curious. The Natural Child is also fearful, self-indulgent, self-centered, rebellious, and aggressive.

Strong basic drives, related to physical survival, are centered in the Natural Child. Yet, in some people the Natural Child is so repressed it is almost blocked off; in others it is overly expressed in inappropriate ways. Either of these extremes can create problems later in life. One of the goals in transactional analysis is learning to become aware of this part of the personality, and to express it appropriately.

EXERCISE 4. RECOGNIZING THE NATURAL CHILD

Describe ways in which the Natural Child might be expressed during the course of a workday or a day at home, or being at a party.

Negatively

at work _____

_____

_____

at home _____

_____

_____

at a party _____

_____

_____

Positively

at work _____

_____

_____

at home _____

_____

_____

at a party _____

_____

_____

THE LITTLE PROFESSOR

The Little Professor is the unschooled wisdom of a child. It is that part of
the Child ego state that is intuitive, manipulative, and creative. When intu-
iting, the Little Professor responds to nonverbal messages and plays hunches.
When using it a child also figures things out, things such as when to cry,
when to be quiet, and how to manipulate mama into smiling.

     Have you ever seen a secretary get what she wants from her boss by using
a quivering chin and teary eyes as she tells him how hard she tries to keep
up with the work? a boss get what he wants from a secretary by sighing,
"My wife just doesn't understand me"? a salesman clinch a deal by saying,
"That car looks as if it were made for you"? If so, you have watched the
manipulative Little Professor at work.

     People who express their creativity purposefully use their Little Profes-
sor in conjunction with their Adult ego state. When a person experiences a
moment of genius, his Little Professor is probably in on it. The Adult and
the Little Professor make a good team. Together they can design a new
building, improve human relationships, create relevant training programs,
develop a mathematical formula, and so forth.

EXERCISE 5. RECOGNIZING THE LITTLE PROFESSOR

Describe ways in which the intuitive, creative, and manipulative Little Professor might be expressed on the job, in a family, or in a classroom.

Negatively

on the job _____

_____

_____

in a family _____

_____

_____

in a classroom _____

_____

_____

Positively

on the job _____

_____

_____

in a family _____

_____

_____

in a classroom _____

_____

_____

THE ADAPTED CHILD IS THE TRAINED CHILD

The Adapted Child is that part of the Child ego state that exhibits a modification of the Natural Child's inclinations. These adaptations of natural impulses occur in response to traumas, experiences, training, and most importantly, to demands from significant authority figures. For example, a child is naturally programmed to eat when hungry. Shortly after birth, however, this natural urge may be adapted so that eating on schedule is determined by the parents.

Children would also do and take what they want <u>naturally</u>, but they may be <u>adapted</u> to share and to be courteous toward others in ways also determined by their parents.

The Adapted Child is likely to do what parents have directed, rational or irrational, and may learn to feel not-OK. Berne says the Adapted Child is like a ventriloquist's dummy. Whereas some adaptation of natural impulses is essential, many children experience training that is unnecessarily repressive. Their natural expressiveness becomes overly inhibited. Common patterns of adaptation are: complying, withdrawing, and procrastinating.

A person who is overly adapted to comply may seek a life career that is routine and shun responsibility.

A person who withdraws as an adaptation may seek a life career in which he or she is isolated from others or rarely speaks to others.

A person who adapted by procrastinating finds it hard to meet deadlines, can't get work done on time, delays starting a project, etc.

EXERCISE 6.   RECOGNIZING THE ADAPTED CHILD

Describe ways the Adapted Child might be expressed on the job, in a family, or in a classroom.

Negatively

on the job _____

_____

_____

in the family _____

_____

_____

in the classroom _____

_____

_____

Positively

on the job _____

_____

_____

in a family _____

_____

_____

in a classroom _____

_____

_____

EXERCISE 7.   GETTING TO KNOW YOUR CHILD EGO STATE

Write three things you do now to express your Natural Child.

_____

_____

_____

Write three things you do now to express your Little Professor.

_____

_____

_____

Write three things you do now to express your Adapted Child.

_____

_____

_____

Think of three recent situations in which you used Child words or behavior.

_____

_____

_____

Was it your Adapted Child, Natural Child, or Little Professor?

_____

Was your behavior similar to things you did or said in your own childhood?

_____

EVERYONE HAS AN ADULT EGO STATE

The Adult ego state can be used to reason, to evaluate stimuli, to gather information, and to store this information for future reference. Furthermore, it enables a person to use these data to make decisions and to implement these decisions. It also enables people to survive independently and to be more selective with their responses.

The Adult gives a person a measure of objectivity. With the Adult a person can examine himself or herself more realistically. He or she can evaluate Parent and Child programming and decide what is all right and what needs to be changed.

By using the Adult a person can reality-test and estimate probabilities. Reality testing is the process of checking out what is real. It involves separating fact from fantasy, traditions, opinions, and archaic feelings. It includes the data to past knowledge and experience. Reality testing allows a person to figure out alternative solutions.

When a person has alternative solutions, probable consequences of the various courses of action can then be estimated, thus minimizing the possibility of failure and regret, and increasing the possibility of creative success.

For example, a person with job dissatisfaction but Parent programmed to "stick with it no matter what" can reality test this value and decide whether or not it is an appropriate response. If the decision to "stick to it no matter what" is not good, alternatives can be searched out on the basis of personal capacities, talents, interests, job opportunities, and so forth. Data can be gathered from a visit to a vocational counselor, job aptitude testing, interviews with personnel managers, studying want-ads, sending for and reading material that will help broaden the knowledge base of career opportunities.

A person can then study what he or she really wants in a job — security, a flexible time schedule, an expense account, travel assignments, regular hours, an intellectual challenge, a chance to be with people, or whatever — and can decide which satisfactions mean the most and what compromises will be made. A person can then select available alternatives, estimate the probable consequences, and adopt a course of action that will render the maximum staisfaction.

THE ADULT CAN BE THE EXECUTIVE OF THE PERSONALITY

The Adult ego state as the executive of the personality referees between the Parent ego state and the Child ego state, especially when the inner dialogue is hurtful or destructive. In such cases the Adult becomes a more rational Parent to the Child than the actual parents were—setting rational limits, giving rational permissions, seeking reasonable gratification for the Child. The following cases indicate how the Adult might referee or effect a compromise between Child and Parent dialogue.

JIM

(C) I'm going to play sick this week and not go to work.

(P) Mommie's boy should stay home if he doesn't feel good.

(A) I could get away with it, but I'd have to work twice as hard to make up for it. No point in staying home.

MARY

(C) If I make good money the men might not like me.

(P) Women shouldn't make as much money as men.

(A) I'm capable, but I'll never get a raise here. I think I'll look for a new job.

The Adult does not always reject the Parent or Child but evaluates Parent and Child behavior and decides what is appropriate to the situation.

The criterion for functioning from the Adult ego state is not based on the correctness of the decisions, but on the process of reality testing and probability estimating by which the decisions are made.

EXERCISE 8. GETTING TO KNOW YOUR ADULT EGO STATE

A. Think of three decisions you recently made. Did you make them on the basis of logical thinking? Parental traditions? Child feelings?

_____

_____

_____

_____

B. How do you use your Adult at work? at home? in learning situations? in social gatherings?

_____

_____

_____

_____

C. Write three illustrations related to the preceding question that are appropriate for class discussion.

_____

_____

_____

_____

EXERCISE 9. EGO STATES AND WRITING

Ego States show in our writing. Read through the following memo and see how.

Then in small groups discuss:

1. the ego state from which this memo is written.

2. the ego state it is likely to activate in the reader.

3. the effectiveness of this memo.

WIN-A-THING MEMO

TO: Area Supervisor
FROM: VIP

Everyone should be excited about our Win-a-Thing Program. We expect X Company employees to encourage their friends, relatives, and customers to take out a new account with us this month and perhaps "win a thing."

As long as X Company is growing and expanding there is no worry for you about your job—even in hard times.

As a loyal employee you should keep things going. Let's grow!

---

4. Now attempt to rewrite the memo using a more straightforward approach. You may wish to relate it to your own organization.

EXERCISE 10.   EGO STATE REACTION QUIZ

Identify each reaction to the situation as either Parent, Adult, or Child (P, A, or C). There will be one of each in each situation. Naturally these will be educated guesses, since you can't hear the tone of voice or see the gestures.

1. A clerk loses an important letter.

   a) "Why can't you keep track of anything you're responsible for?" _____

   b) "Check each person who may have used it in the last two days and try to trace it. Perhaps Mrs. Smith can help you." _____

   c) "I can't solve your problems. I didn't take your old letter." _____

2. A piece of equipment breaks down.

   a) "See if a repairman can come this morning." _____

   b) "Wow! This machine is always breaking down. I'd like to throw it on the floor and jump on it." _____

   c) "Those operators are so careless. They should know better." _____

3. The boss is not satisfied with a letter his secretary wrote in reply to a memo from another department.

   a) "Golly, Mr. Smith, I read that memo three times and it's so bad I just can't figure it out. He must be a jerk." _____

   b) "I found the memo contradictory, Mr. Smith. I'd appreciate your telling me what you see as his main question." _____

   c) "We shouldn't have to answer this memo at all. That man clearly doesn't know what he's talking about." _____

4. Coffee break rumors report a co-worker is about to be transferred.

   a) "Boy, tell me more. I'd like to get something on George. He gives me a pain in the neck!" _____

   b) "Let's not spread a story that may not be true. If we have a question, let's ask the boss." _____

   c) "We really shouldn't talk about poor old George. He has so many troubles—financial, marital, you name it." _____

5. The boss has had an important proposal rejected.

   a) "Poor Mr. Brown, you must feel terrible. I'll fix you a
cup of tea to cheer you up."   _____

   b) "You think you feel bad! Just listen to what happened
to me!"   _____

   c) "I'm sorry about the reversal, Mr. Brown. Let me
know if there is anything you want me to do."   _____

6. A buxom secretary appears on the job in a very tight sweater.

   a) "Wow, look at that!"   _____

   b) "Tight sweaters should not be allowed in the office."   _____

   c) "I wonder why she chose that to wear to work."   _____

7. Someone unexpectedly gets a promotion.

   a) "Well, Mrs. White deserved it. After all, with all those
children to feed, she needs that extra money. Poor thing."   _____

   b) "Oh, brother! She got that for buttering up the higher-ups."   _____

   c) "I thought I was more qualified for the promotion than
Mrs. White. But maybe I haven't given her enough credit."   _____

8. A reduction in personnel is announced.

   a) "What will I do if I'm laid off?"   _____

   b) "This damn company isn't worth working for anyway."   _____

   c) "I believe that all women should be fired first. They don't
need the money. They're just taking jobs away from men."   _____

Participants may differ in responses but can defend their responses. However, here are our suggestions.

1. P A C   3. C A P   5. P C A   7. C A P

2. C A P   4. P A C   6. P C A   8. P C A

SUMMARY

People have an image of their parent figures, though they may
not be their actual parents. These form the Parent ego state.
At times, any person can use actions, words, gestures, and
opinions from the Parent ego state. At other times, the Child
ego state listens to a reply of these inner Parent messages
whether they are positive or not.
     Every child is born with inherited characteristics, born
into a specific social, economic, and emotional environment,
and trained in certain ways by authority figures. Every
child experiences significant events such as death in the
family, illness, pain, accidents, geographical dislocation,
and economic crisis. These influences contribute to the
uniqueness of childhood for each person and form the Child
ego state. No two children, even in the same family, have the
same childhood.
     Every person has an Adult ego state which if used can deal
objectively with reality. The Adult ego state is not related
to age but is influenced by education and experience. When
it is activated, a person can collect and organize information,
predict possible consequences or various actions, and make
conscious decisions. Even though a decision is made from the
Adult, it is not necessarily accurate if information is lacking.
However, using the Adult can help to minimize regrettable
actions and can increase a person's potential for success.
     You have three different ego states programmed with
different behavior. Begin to be aware of when you are coming
on Parent, Adult, or Child. Awareness gives you more choice
in your communication patterns and in setting your life goals.

UNIT 3. THE TRANSACTIONS PEOPLE USE

Do you know people who when they talk to others seem to be on the same wavelength?

Do you know people who when they talk to others seem to shut off the conversation?

Do you know people who do not talk straight, who say one thing but mean another?

If so, you have observed the three basic types of transactions that occur whenever two or more people are together. These transactions are complementary, crossed, and ulterior.

Anything that happens between people involves a stimulus and a response. These are interpersonal transactions and occur between one or more ego states of one person and one or more ego states of another. For example, the stimulus may be sent from the Child in one to the Child in another, from the Adult in one to the Adult in another, from the Child in one to the Parent in another, and so on.

SOME TRANSACTIONS ARE COMPLEMENTARY

A complementary transaction occurs when a message, sent from one ego state, gets the expected response from a specific ego state in the other person. In this case the lines of communication are open.

For example:

Sender   Responder

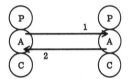

1. "Do you know where the Simpson report is?"

2. "It seems to be temporarily misplaced. I have a tracer out on it."

The same initial question can be asked with a minor change of words, and different gestures, facial expression, tone of voice, etc., and elicit a different response. For example, a stimulus originating in one person's Child ego state frequently brings out the Parent ego state in another.

Sender   Responder

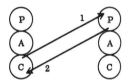

1. (With a worried look) "Do you know where the Simpson report is?"

2. (Sympathetically) "Now don't you worry. I have a tracer out on it right now."

Or it may activate the Child in another:

Sender   Responder

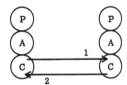

1. (Angrily kicking the leg of the desk) "Do you know where that damn Simpson report is?"

2. "I've spent an hour looking for that blasted thing, too. Sure is maddening."

If a verbal message is to be completely understood, both the sender and the receiver must take into consideration the nonverbal aspects as well as the spoken words. Gestures, facial expressions, body posture, tone of voice, and so forth, all contribute to the meaning in every transaction, and lines of communication remain open if the response is an expected one.

To understand another person's meaning is to enhance relationships. Understanding lifts morale and contributes to the kind of atmosphere where work and family relations can be more pleasurable.

EXERCISE 1. ANALYZING COMPLEMENTARY TRANSACTIONS

Develop dialogue that fits the following diagrams. Describe the behavior if necessary for clarification. Use illustrations from your organization, classroom, or family.

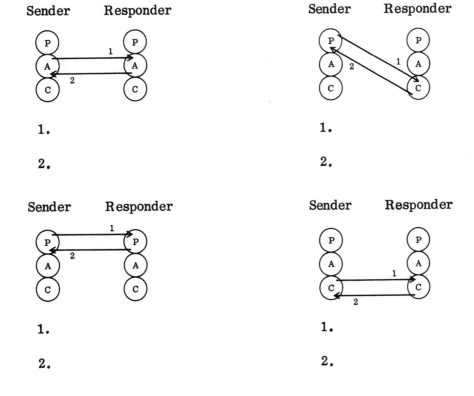

Sender   Responder

1.

2.

Sender   Responder

1.

2.

Sender   Responder

1.

2.

Sender   Responder

1.

2.

Note to leader: Slides showing a situation — facial expressions, postures, gestures, etc. — could be developed to complement this exercise.

SOME TRANSACTIONS ARE CROSSED

Crossed transactions are a frequent source of resentment between people.
When two people stand glaring at each other, turn their backs on each other,
are unwilling to continue transacting, or are puzzled by what has just
occurred between them, it is likely that they have just experienced a <u>crossed</u>
<u>transaction</u>.

For example:

Sender   Responder

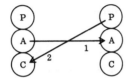

1. "Do you know where the dictionary is?"

2. (Critically) "It's right where you left it.
    Can't you remember anything?"

Sender   Responder

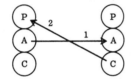

1. "Do you know where the dictionary is?"

2. (Whining) "Why ask me? I never use that
    thing."

Sender   Responder

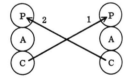

1. "Please help me find the dictionary. I'm
    so tired."

2. "Well, I'm tired, too. I was out late last
    night."

Crossed transactions occur whenever an unexpected response is made to
the stimulus. An ego state is activated unexpectedly and the lines of transacting between the people are crossed. At this point, people tend to withdraw, turn away from each other, or switch the conversation in another
direction.

EXERCISE 2. ANALYZING CROSSED TRANSACTIONS

Develop dialogue that fits the following crossed diagrams. Describe behavior if necessary for clarification. Use illustrations from your organization, classroom, or family.

Sender   Responder

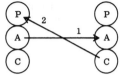

1.

2.

Sender   Responder

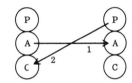

1.

2.

Sender   Responder

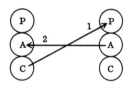

1.

2.

Sender   Responder

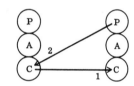

1.

2.

SOME TRANSACTIONS ARE ULTERIOR

Ulterior transactions occur on the job, at home, and when
shopping, as well as when attending social functions. Ulterior
transactions have a hidden agenda. The hidden agenda is like
a double message. This ulterior message is more important to
the sender and to the receiver than are the overt, verbal transactions. (Ulterior transactions are diagrammed with a dotted
line.)

If a car salesperson says to a customer with a leer, "This
is our finest sports car, but it may be too racy for you,"
the message being sent can be heard either by the customer's
Adult ego state or by the Child ego state (see the figure
below). If the customer's Adult hears, the response may be,
"Yes, you're right, considering the requirements of my job."
From the Child, the response might be, "I'll take it. It's
just what I want."

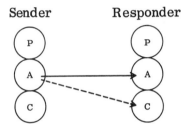

An ulterior message is also given when a secretary submits
a letter to the boss with several typing errors. This invites
the boss to give the secretary a Parental put-down (see the
figure below). The same happens when a student is continually
late with assignments, absent from class, writes illegibly, or
in some way provokes the equivalent of parental criticism.

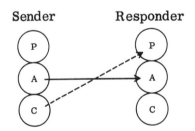

Other ulterior messages may be sent by:

A child who suddenly limps, trying to get out of running
an errand for his or her mother, is sending the message
"I'm too helpless to walk to the store."

Or a person who looks downcast, refuses to speak, and
sighs deeply, saying, "You don't really love me or you'd
finish this work."

Ulterior messages are the heart of all psychological games
(games will be discussed more fully in a later unit). For

example, if a woman plays a game of Rapo, she baits a man with sexy behavior (Child to Child ulterior), perhaps while they are discussing a recent news item (plausible Adult to Adult transaction), then cuts him down when he reaches for the bait. Her ulterior message is "I'm available," even though she has no intention of being available.   Instead she wants to prove an early childhood decision, "Men are not-OK."   Men play the same game.

A similar ulterior transaction occurs when a man "butters up" a woman and then drops her cold when she responds.

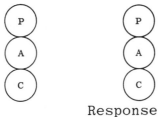

EXERCISE 3.   ANALYZING ULTERIOR TRANSACTIONS

Study the entire message in the following two illustrations. Diagram the surface transaction and the ulterior transaction.

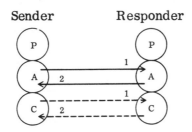

Stimulus

1. "Here's that report."

2. Ulterior transaction: wiggles hips, meaning "See how sexy I am."

Response

3. "Thank you."

4. Ulterior transaction: stares with appreciation meaning "I'm interested."

 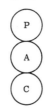

Stimulus

1. "Sorry this is late."

2. Ulterior transaction: sighs, meaning "Kick me. I'm bad."

Response

3. "It's too late to be graded."

4. Ulterior transaction: frowns, meaning "OK, here's your kick."

EXERCISE 4. TRANSACTIONAL RESPONSES

Design possible ego state responses to these situations.

Situation 1

A co-worker comes to work blurry-eyed and tired.

Parent _____

_____

_____

Adult _____

_____

_____

Child _____

_____

_____

Which of the above transactions are complementary? Which are crossed?
Which are ulterior?

Situation 2

You are given a deadline to meet that is extremely demanding and difficult.

Parent _____

_____

_____

Adult _____

_____

_____

Child _____

_____

_____

Which of the above transactions are complementary? Which are crossed?
Which are ulterior?

Situation 3

Someone else has made an error and you are calling attention to it.

Parent _____

_____

_____

Adult _____

_____

_____

Child _____

_____

_____

Situation 4

Now work in small groups to design important communication problems and situations in your particular organization. Then develop possible Parent, Adult, and Child responses to each of these situations. (You may wish to take each situation in turn and group participants in Group 1 – Parent, Group 2 – Adult, Group 3 – Child. Switch group ego status when you move on to the next situation).

Situation

_____

_____

Possible ego state responses

P _____

_____

A _____

_____

C _____

_____

EXERCISE 5.   MULTIPLE-CHOICE RESPONSES

To do this exercise check the response that is nearest to the way you would react. Try to work quickly, giving your initial response.

Situation 1

You are planning a new business venture but the planning is not yet complete. A co-worker, speaking from the Parent ego state, asks "What's going on here?" You would:

_____ 1.   Tell the person all about it.

_____ 2.   Ask the person what information is wanted.

_____ 3.   Change the subject.

_____ 4.   Tell the person you're thinking of making a change but have not completed your plans.

_____ 5.   Wink or give the person a sly look.

_____ 6.   (Other) _____

Situation 2

Your superior issues instructions loudly while frowning and banging on his desk as his or her father used to do. The instructions, if followed, will result in the company's losing money. You would:

_____ 1.   Follow instructions and not say anything.

_____ 2.   Point out the error but follow instructions anyway.

_____ 3.   Do what is said and tell others about the error in judgment.

_____ 4.   Explain why the loss will result.

_____ 5.   Argue with your superior.

_____ 6.   (Other) _____

Situation 3

Someone with less seniority who's always fooling around gets the promotion you were working for.   You would:

_____   1. Talk to the boss about it.

_____   2. Complain to your other co-workers.

_____   3. Feel depressed but stay silent.

_____   4. Be angry about it and take out your anger on someone at home.

_____   5. Start to avoid the person who gets the promotion.

_____   6. (Other) _____

Situation 4

You have an important date for the evening, then someone in your office takes off with an unexpected illness. The boss has no other alternative but to ask you to stay late and complete the extra work. You would:

_____   1. Object strongly and refuse to do it.

_____   2. Object strongly, then say you'll do it.

_____   3. Comply silently.

_____   4. Feel sorry for yourself and look downcast.

_____   5. Cancel your date because you were "glad to help out."

_____   6. (Other) _____

Situation 5

Your friend buys a new car, the kind you always wanted. You would:

_____   1. Sulk silently.

_____   2. Try to outdo him by getting a better one for yourself.

_____   3. Comment on the car's weak points.

_____   4. Be pleased and ask to be taken for a ride.

_____   5. Find out all you can about it.

_____   6. (Other) _____

Now look back at the responses you checked.

1. Draw two sets of three circles beside each situation. Label them Parent, Adult, and Child.

2. Draw lines indicating which ego state the stimulus came from in each situation.

3. Next draw lines showing your responses.

4. How many of your responses were complementary? _____
    crossed? _____   ulterior? _____

EXERCISE 6. DESIGNING YOUR OWN TRANSACTIONS

Working with your group, design four complementary transactions that are
common to your everyday life.

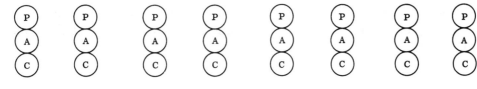

1.   1.   1.   1.

2.   2.   2.   2.

Working with your group, design four crossed transactions that are common
to your everyday life.

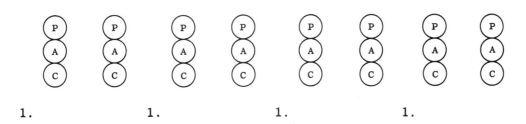

1.   1.   1.   1.

2.   2.   2.   2.

Working with your group, design four ulterior transactions that are common
to your everyday life.

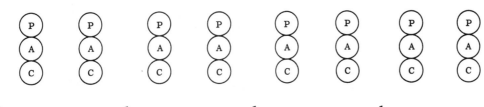

1.   1.   1.   1.

2.   2.   2.   2.

SUMMARY

In interpersonal relations the unit of measure is the transaction. By analyzing transactions people can gain a conscious control of how they operate with others. They can determine when transactions are complementary, crossed, or ulterior.

In healthy relationships people transact directly, straightforwardly, and, on occasion, intensely. These transactions tend to be complementary and free from ulterior motives.

EXTRA TRANSACTIONAL DIAGRAMS

These pages are for your convenience for further exploration of typical transactions in your organization.

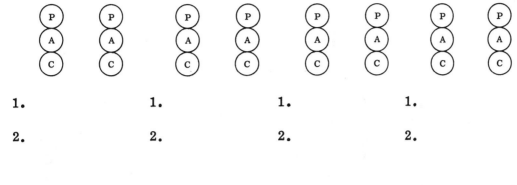

1.   1.   1.   1.

2.   2.   2.   2.

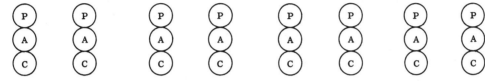

1.   1.   1.   1.

2.   2.   2.   2.

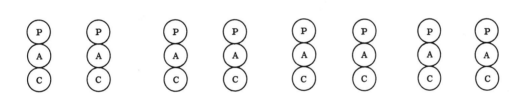

1.   1.   1.   1.

2.   2.   2.   2.

P   P   P   P   P   P   P   P
A   A   A   A   A   A   A   A
C   C   C   C   C   C   C   C

1.   1.   1.   1.
2.   2.   2.   2.

P   P   P   P   P   P   P   P
A   A   A   A   A   A   A   A
C   C   C   C   C   C   C   C

1.   1.   1.   1.
2.   2.   2.   2.

P   P   P   P   P   P   P   P
A   A   A   A   A   A   A   A
C   C   C   C   C   C   C   C

1.   1.   1.   1.
2.   2.   2.   2.

P A C   P A C   P A C   P A C   P A C   P A C   P A C   P A C

1.   1.   1.   1.
2.   2.   2.   2.

P A C   P A C   P A C   P A C   P A C   P A C   P A C   P A C

1.   1.   1.   1.
2.   2.   2.   2.

P A C   P A C   P A C   P A C   P A C   P A C   P A C   P A C

1.   1.   1.   1.
2.   2.   2.   2.

UNIT 4. STROKES AND THE PSYCHOLOGICAL TRADING STAMPS
PEOPLE COLLECT

Do you know someone who holds resentments and then blows up at a slight provocation?

Do you know someone who rejects compliments when they're given?

Do you know someone who shows appreciation and is a pleasure to be around?

If you do, you have observed people giving and receiving positive, negative, and counterfeit strokes (any form of touch or recognition) which later result in psychological trading stamp collections (a collection of good and/or bad feelings).

Every person has the need to be touched and to be recognized by other people.   These are biological and psychological needs which can be thought of as "hungers."

The hungers for touch and recognition can be appeased with strokes which are "any act implying recognition of another's presence."[1]   Strokes can be given in the form of actual physical touch or by some symbolic form of recognition such as a look, a word, a gesture, or any act that says "I know you're there."

PEOPLE NEED STROKES TO SURVIVE

Infants will not grow normally without the touch of others. Something about being touched stimulates an infant's chemistry for mental and phsyical growth.   Among transactional analysts there is a saying, "If the infant is not stroked, the spinal cord shrivels up."[2]   Infants who are neglected, ignored, or for any reason do not experience enough touch suffer mental and physical deterioration even to the point of death.

As a child grows older, the early primary hunger for actual physical touch is modified and becomes recognition hunger.   A smile, a nod, a word, a frown, a gesture begin to substitute for some touch strokes.   Like touch, these forms of recognition, whether positive or negative, stimulate the brain of the ones receiving them and serve to verify for them the fact that they are there and alive.   Recognition strokes also keep their nervous system from "shriveling."

While either negative or positive strokes may stimulate an infant's body chemistry, it takes positive strokes to develop emotionally healthy persons with a sense of OKness. The lack of sufficient strokes always has a detrimental effect on people.

Positive strokes leave the person feeling good, alive, alert, and significant.   At a greater depth they enhance the individual's sense of well-being, endorse a person's intelligence, and are often pleasurable.   The feelings beneath positive strokes are feelings of goodwill and convey the I'm OK, You're OK position.

Stroke hunger can be strongly felt anywhere, even on the job.   In an industrial situation a supervisor complained that one of the lab workers was spending too much time at the water cooler leaving the lab isolated every hour looking for someone to talk to. The supervisor, after being trained in TA, made it a practice to check into the lab at intervals for a brief friendly conversation with this worker.   The trips into the hallway diminished considerably.   As this supervisor discovered, the varying human needs for recognition confront anyone who works with people.   Effective managers are often those who are able to touch and recognize others appropriately.

EXERCISE 1.   ANALYZING STROKES AND RECOGNITION

With your group, develop a list of verbal and/or nonverbal strokes that may be given in the home, at work, or in the classroom.

Negative Strokes

in the home _____

_____

_____

at work _____

_____

_____

in the classroom _____

_____

_____

Positive Strokes

in the home _____

_____

_____

at work _____

_____

_____

in the classroom _____

_____

_____

PEOPLE COLLECT GOOD AND BAD FEELINGS

Collecting a good feeling from a positive stroke is collecting a "psychological gold stamp." Collecting a bad feeling from a negative stroke is collecting a psychological "gray" stamp (or brown stamp, as some prefer). In transactional analysis the good or bad feelings a person collects are called "trading stamps." The term "stamps" is borrowed from the practice in some parts of the country of collecting trading stamps when making purchases and later redeeming them for merchandise. [3]

Specific color is sometimes assigned a stamp to represent a bad feeling: red stamps for anger, blue stamps for hurt feelings and depression, white stamps for purity and self-righteousness, green stamps for jealousy and envy, etc.

The color assigned to psychological trading stamps is, of course, unimportant. The important point is the fact that pscyhological trading stamps represent an indulgence in bad feelings learned in childhood which are saved up and eventually "redeemed."

PREFERRED COLLECTIONS START IN CHILDHOOD

Children are not born with their feelings already programmed toward objects and people. Each child learns toward whom and toward what affection can be shown. Each learns toward who and about what to feel guilty. Each learns whom and what to fear. Each learns whom and what to hate. Each learns how to give and receive certain kinds of strokes.

Although children experience all feelings, they eventually adapt with a learned feeling that they come to prefer as their "favorite" feeling. This is what was commonly felt when things "got tough" around the house.

A child who continually hears "I'm ashamed of you!" or "You should be ashamed of yourself!" learns to collect fear stamps.

A child who continually hears "Just wait until your father gets home; he'll beat you good" learns to collect fear stamps.

A child who continually hears "Don't speak to those people; they can't be trusted" learns to collect anger or suspicion stamps.

A child who continually hears "What's the matter with you! Can't you do anything right!" learns to collect stupid stamps.

While these feelings may have been an understandable response to the original childhood situations, later in life a person tends to seek similar situations to give and get a particular stroke so that old feelings can be reexperienced. A negative stamp collection is formed from these feelings that seem familiar. For example, a person who in childhood takes the position, "I'm stupid", later does stupid things to rein-force the old "I'm stupid" belief.

To collect more negative stamps, a person can manipulate others who will in return hurt, belittle, cause anger,

frighten, or arouse guilt, etc. This is accomplished by pro-
voking or inviting others to play certain roles or by <u>imagining</u>
that something has been inflicted by another person.
     Children who learn to feel OK about themselves and others
learn to collect and give gold stamps. They direct their
energies toward constructive behavior that give them good
feelings about themselves and others.

EXERCISE 2.   GIVING AND RECEIVING GOOD AND BAD FEELINGS

Read over the following. What are bad feelings that could be
given or received? State at least three examples. (These
situations could be role-played.)

Situation 1

A teller gives a customer the bank balance. The customer
thinks it may be wrong and is critical. Thus the teller feels
bad. (State dialogue and/or body language.)

_____

_____

_____

Teller is critical of the customer who then responds because
of negative feelings. (State dialogue and/or body language.)

_____

_____

_____

Now use the same situations and change them to illustrate the
giving and receiving of good feelings.

Customer:_____

_____

_____

Teller:_____

_____

_____

Situation 2

A manager discusses a performance report with one of the supervisors.
The manager feels the supervisor is a good employee but needs to pay closer
attention to human relationship problems. For one thing, he is suggesting
the supervisor study transactional analysis.

Manager giving bad feelings (gray stamps) to supervisor (state dialogue and/
or body language).

_____

_____

_____

Supervisor giving bad feelings (gray stamps) to manager (state dialogue and/
or body language).

_____

_____

_____

Now do the same with each, only give at least three illustrations of giving
good feelings (gold stamps).

Manager: _____

_____

_____

Supervisor: _____

_____

_____

Situation 3

Now design a specific communications situation typical of your family or the organization in which you work.

_____

_____

_____

How can bad feelings (gray stamps) be given in this situation?

_____

_____

_____

How can good feelings (gold stamps) be given in this situation?

_____

_____

_____

EXERCISE 3.   STAMP COLLECTING

The class first decides on a topic suitable for an interview
by two participants that is relevant to the group, i.e.,
flight manager discussing an overweight problem with stewardess,
supervisor discussing a performance report or tardiness
counseling, late college papers, etc.

The interview can be set up between two class participants
with 8 or 10 participants watching as in a "fishbowl."
Participants have a stack of gold and a stack of gray stamps
in front of them. As the discussion ensues, each participant
puts a gray or gold stamp toward the other person if he or
she feels that a "good" or "bad" feeling is being given.
Each also takes a gray or gold stamp from the pile if the
feeling received from the other is "good" or "bad".

Allow at least 10 minutes for the interview and 10
minutes for group discussion after the interview.

STAMPS ARE EVENTUALLY CASHED IN

People eventually cash in their bad feelings. Have you
ever seen a put-down collected and passed down a chain of
command? For example, a department manager may receive a
negative stroke from a spouse before leaving for work in the
morning. No resolution of the problem is made. Bad feelings
are collected and carried off to work. At work they are
cashed in on one of the supervisors with, "What's the matter
with you? I expected this report at 9 A.M., not 10 A.M.!"
The supervisor collects bad feelings and takes them back to
the secretary to cash in. "Didn't you see that note I left?
Why can't you get things to me on time? I also found several
typing errors in that last report." The secretary goes home
and cashes in on a spouse. "Why haven't you finished that
painting job? The place looks a mess—as usual!" The spouse
turns to the children with, "You can't do anything right. Look
at the stuff you've left around for all of us to stumble over!"
The children may cash in by kicking the dog!

The process of stamp collection and redemption is:

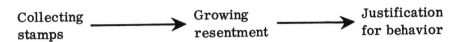

Collecting stamps ⟶ Growing resentment ⟶ Justification for behavior

People acquire collections of different sizes and have different compulsions as to when, where, and how to redeem their negative collections. Some people collect the equivalent of a page of stamps and turn them in for relatively small prizes: having a headache, throwing an eraser, dropping a typewriter, dressing-down an employee, spilling a file drawer, or mailing a letter in the wrong envelope.

For some, however, the prize is somewhat bigger. If they have saved several "books" of gray stamps, they then feel justified when they do such things as wreck an office machine, injure themselves, have a guilt-free affair, take company property, fire a valued employee, stay home "sick," arrive at work late several times in a row, and so forth.

Occasionally people save an even larger collection, cashing it in for a larger prize: a mental breakdown, imprisonment, dropping out of society, or losing a valued job.

When a person has collected enough stamps and is ready to cash them in, words and/or phrases are often used to indicate that redemption time is at hand:

> That's the last straw!
> I've taken all I'm going to!
> I've had it up to here!
> Dear John ...

If a person collects enough good feelings from others, there is justification for doing something personally rewarding. Gold stamps can be cashed in to go out to dinner, buy a new suit, have a fun weekend, or take a pleasant vacation.

EXERCISE 4. CASHING-IN TIME

What are other possible words, phrases, body messages that could indicate a pile of resentment is about to be redeemed? Develop at least three.

_____

_____

_____

_____

What are possible words, phrases, and body messages that could indicate many gold stamps were about to be redeemed?

_____

_____

_____

_____

EXERCISE 5.   YOUR NEGATIVE STAMP COLLECTION

Try to recall at least two situations in the last week in which you collected and held a negative feeling.

What was the situation? _____

_____

_____

Who was involved? _____

_____

_____

What feeling(s) did you collect? _____

_____

_____

Do you still hold resentment over either or both of these situations?

_____

When you have "taken enough" from people, how do you cash-in? Who or what do you cash in on?

_____

_____

Now explore alternatives to "taking it." Could you have handled the situation a different way so that you didn't collect?

_____

_____

Try to discover any pattern of stamp collecting and redeeming that you have learned from your past experiences that may be a hindrance to you now.

_____

_____

EXERCISE 6. YOUR GOLD STAMP COLLECTION

Recall during the past two weeks at least two situations in which you received positive strokes and collected gold stamps. What was the situation?

_____

_____

_____

Who was involved? _____

_____

_____

How did you feel? _____

_____

_____

Does the memory of it make you feel good now? _____

_____

_____

What good things do you do for yourself when you cash in gold stamps?

_____

_____

_____

_____

Over the next week attempt to be conscious of your collections of good and bad feelings. Make your gold stamp collection larger. Diminish your negative stamp collection.

SUMMARY

Everyone needs strokes to survive and to maintain a sense of well-being. Environments that are void of good strokes are sterile, and motivation and productivity go down.

Feelings are often adapted in childhood. You may have been taught to respond with a preferred negative feeling—fear, guilt, anger, inadequacy, etc.—when things went wrong in your family. Later this feeling is unconsciously sought after. In fact, one of the reasons psychological games are played is to give and receive negative stamps.

Psychological gray (or brown) stamps—bad feelings—can be collected and held and then cashed-in for an unpleasant prize. Good feelings about yourself—gold stamps—can also be collected and redeemed for a pleasant prize.

UNIT 5.   THE GAMES PEOPLE PLAY

Do you know someone who often gets picked on?

Do you know someone who often does the picking?

Do you know someone who often tries to intervene?

If you do, then you have observed the basic roles of Victim,
Persecutor, and Rescuer [1] being played in psychological games.

People play psychological games with one another that have
maneuvers similar to games like monopoly, bridge, or checkers
that people play at social gatherings. In any game the players
must know the game in order to play — after all, if one person
enters a card party ready to play bridge, and everyone else is
playing pinochle, this person can't very well play bridge.

PSYCHOLOGICAL GAMES HAVE NEGATIVE PAYOFFS

People play psychological games — often in an unaware way — and
tend to choose a spouse, friends, and even business associates
those people who will play the role opposite their own.
Although there are many different games, in each one there
are three basic elements:

  1. A series of complementary transactions which on the
      surface seem plausible.

  2. An ulterior transaction which is the hidden agenda.

  3. A negative payoff which concludes the game and is the
      real purpose for playing.

Games tend to be repetitious. People find themselves saying
the same words in the same way, only the time and place may
change. Perhaps the replay contributes to what is often
described as "I feel as if I've done this before."

People play games with different degrees of intensity — from
the socially accepted relaxed level, such as flirting with a
gentle brushoff at a cocktail party, to the criminal homicide/
suicide level, such as criminal assault and rape. Games are
like short scenes in a life drama.

IT TAKES MORE THAN ONE TO PLAY A GAME

Even as some people have favorite ego states, they also have a favorite game role. Games may involve either two or three of the dramatic roles of Victim, Persecutor, and Rescuer — the manipulative roles learned in childhood. Games played from the Persecutor or Rescuer roles serve to reinforce a negative position about others — You're not-OK (you need to be punished or rescued). Games from the Victim role serve to reinforce a negative position about oneself — I'm not-OK (I need you to punish me or rescue me).

Each game has its roles, its number of players, its level of intensity, its length, and its ulterior message which is a put-down to oneself or others. Each game has its own dramatic style and can be played in different settings.

Games prevent honest, intimate, and open relationships between the players. Yet people play them because they fill up time, provoke attention, provide a way of getting and giving strokes, reinforce early opinions about self and others, and fulfill a sense of identity and destiny which is characteristic of a psychological script.

THE GAME OF YES, BUT

The game is likely to be Yes, But if the chairperson in a business meeting presents a problem and then shoots down all suggestions. Or if a principal does the same with the teachers at a faculty meeting. Or if a person rejects the helpful suggestions solicited from friends. A person who plays Yes, But does so to maintain a position such as "nobody's going to tell me what to do" or "people are stupid." In childhood if parents try to give all the answers or none at all, a stand is often taken against them (you're not-OK).

To initiate this game Yes, But one player presents a problem in the guise of soliciting advice from one or more other players. If hooked, the other player advises "Why don't you...?" The initiator discounts all suggestions with "Yes, but ...," followed by "reasons" why the advice won't work. Eventually the "why don't you" advice-givers give up and fall silent. This is the payoff of the game to prove the position "parents can't tell me anything" or "parents are stupid."

In this game the Child ego state "hooks" the Nurturing
Parent in the other players. Although the transactions may
appear to be Adult to Adult on the surface ("I've got a
problem. Tell me the answer"), the ulterior transaction is
Child to Parent ("I've got a problem. Just try to tell me
the answer. I won't let you"). Yes, but can be diagrammed
as follows:

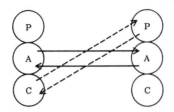

Sender: "I've got a problem..."   Responder: "Why don't you..."

THE GAME OF KICK ME

In a game of Kick Me the player does something to provoke
another player to put him down.

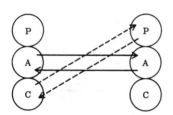

Subordinate: "I stayed up too late
last night and didn't
make the sale this
morning." (ulterior:
I'm a bad person,
kick me.)

Boss: "Sorry about that.
This is the last day
I can give a bonus
for that sale."
(ulterior: Yes, you
are a bad person and
here is your kick.)

   Though it may be denied, a person who is used to the game
of Kick Me tends to attract others who can play the complementary hand and are willing to give the "kick".

THE GAME OF HARRIED

Harried is a common game acted out to justify collapsing or feeling depressed. An executive who plays Harried says "Yes" to everything, volunteers to come early and work late, takes on weekend assignments and carries work home in a briefcase — perhaps even studying it on the commuter bus. For a period of time the harried executive acts like a superperson, but eventually this harried state is reflected externally or internally. Clothes may become disheveled, eyes bloodshot, and personal grooming forgotten. Work goes unfinished. The harried person's mental and physical health deteriorates. So many feelings of depression are collected and saved that collapse is inevitable, and functioning is impaired. Other variations of this game are Harried Housewife, Harried School Teacher, Harried Student, Harried Waitress, Harried Bank Teller, etc.

THE GAME OF SEE WHAT YOU MADE ME DO

A game which is sometimes played to collect anger stamps is See What You Made Me Do. This game is played in the office if a typist makes a mistake while the supervisor is watching from behind. Rather than taking responsibility for the error, the typist turns to the supervisor and angrily says, See What You Made Me Do!, thus, collecting an anger stamp by blaming someone else for the mistake. If this happens often enough, the supervisor may collect fear or guilt stamps and leave the typist alone. In this way the purpose of the game is fulfilled — isolation. Another See What You Made Me Do player may collect feelings of purity instead of anger, "After all, it's not my fault. It's your fault I made my mistake. I'm pure."

THE GAME OF LUNCH BAG

Lunch Bag is a favorite game of executives who are purity and self-righteousness stamp collectors. When an executive plays this game, he or she uses a self-righteous position to manipulate and control others. For example, this person brings a lunch of last night's leftovers in a paper bag and makes an issue of eating in the office while others go out for lunch.

  In such a case the executive wards off the "frivolous" demands of others. The ulterior message given is that "if a big person like me can be this frugal, so can you." Others may feel too guilty or too fearful to approach with their requests.

THE GAME OF STUPID

A game which may be played to collect gray or brown stamps is Stupid. This is played when a secretary "accidentally" puts a letter in a bottom drawer, then later when it's rediscovered makes a fuss, complaining, "How could I have done such a stupid thing? This was that letter that you wanted in Washington, D.C. last month."

OTHER POPULAR GAMES

Themes of other games that are often easily recognized are the following:

Cornered:

"I'm damned if I do and damned if I don't."

Blemish:

"You're fine except for a minor blemish—length of hair, style of clothes, etc., which really spoils everything."

I'm Only Trying
To Help You:

"My advice is so good, why do you want to think for yourself and reject my ideas when I'm only trying to help you?"

Wooden Leg:

"Surely you can't expect much from me when I have such a handicap — i.e., wrong sex, wrong size, wrong race, wrong background, etc."

See How Hard
I Tried:

"Don't blame me if things turn out wrong. After all, see how hard I tried."

Uproar:

"I'm stronger than you are. You stupid fool; you never do anything right."

Now I've Got You,
You S.O.B.:

"I've caught you making a mistake and will now make you suffer!"

EXERCISE 1. DISCOVERING GAMES

Take time to discuss with your group how each of the games mentioned above is played in your organization, in your family, or whatever group is relevant to you (i.e., church, classroom). If a particular game does not seem to apply, go on to the next one. For each game discuss:

- What role is the game likely to be initiated from?

- What kinds of feelings are collected by the parties involved in the games?

- Do some of these games seem to fit together? If so, which ones?

EXERCISE 2. ROLE-PLAYING GAMES

In small groups select two or three of the games from your discussion during Exercise 1. Discuss the specific situations, characterizations, dialogue, setting, and so forth in which these games take place. Develop a dramatic replay of the games. Choose the players. Rehearse. Role-play the games for the entire group.

After each presentation, allow the audience to guess which game(s) was portrayed.

GIVING UP GAMES

In order to give up games, people need to become aware of the games they personally initiate. Once games are recognized and the roles played in them identified, the games can be interrupted, avoided, and then eventually given up instead. Positive strokes can then be given and accepted. Time in the here and now is structured more appropriately. People can devote energies to getting in touch with their capabilities and developing their potentials rather than acting the parts that the games require.

  Games may be foiled by a refusal to play the expected hand or a refusal to give a payoff. For example, refusing to give advice or suggestions to a Yes, But player usually stops the game. There are many ways to stop a game. A person may:

- Give an unexpected response.

- Stop exaggerating his/her own weaknesses or strengths.

- Give and receive positive strokes - gold stamps - rather than negative strokes - gray stamps.

- Structure more of his/her time with activities, intimacy, and fun.

- Stop playing Rescuer — helping those who don't need help.

- Stop playing Persecuter — criticizing those who don't need it.

- Stop playing Victim — acting helpless or dependent when really able to stand on his or her own feet.

EXERCISE 3. STOPPING GAMES

Try an instant replay of several of the games you have already role-played. Select two or three that arouse the greatest interest. Start the game as you did before, but this time break it up in some way. Remember that a game can be stopped from either side.

SUMMARY

Games are negative scenes in life dramas. People play games to reinforce old childhood decisions and to act out their psychological scripts. A game player, as well as getting stamps, gets stroking (though it may be negative), structures his time (though it may be a waste), reinforces his psychological positions (though they may be irrational), furthers his script (though it may be destructive), feels justified in cashing in old resentments (though he over-indulges himself), and avoids authentic encounter (though he may be acting as if that's what he wants). Games can be given up. More positive strokes can be sought. The script can be rewritten.

Do you know someone who constantly acts dependent, authoritarian, or objective?

Do you know someone who seems to be highly prejudiced, has "made up his mind and doesn't want to be confused by the facts"?

Do you know someone who says he hears voices or one who is obviously deluded, unable to separate fact from fantasy?

Do you know someone whose emotions keep him from solving his problems?

Do you know someone who faces the facts and solves his problems constructively?

If you do, you have seen the kind of behavior that is the result of defects in ego state boundaries and the kind of behavior that is the result of a person using Adult executive control.

Berne suggests ego boundaries can be thought of as semi-permeable membranes through which psychic energy can flow from one ego state to another. [1] Ego boundaries must be semi-permeable; otherwise psychic energy would be bound up in one ego state and unable to move about spontaneously as situations change.

In some highly effective people the flow of energy may be quite rapid; in others it may be sluggish. The person whose free energy moves rapidly may be exciting and stimulating, but others may have difficulty keeping up with the fast-moving pace. The one whose energy moves more slowly is the person who is slow to start activities, and slow to stop them. Other people may become impatient with this slowness though the responses may be of high quality.

PEOPLE MAY HAVE FAVORITE EGO STATES

When people are always predictable, the problem is that one or two of their ego state boundaries have become rigid. They have excluded part of their personalities.

If people use only their Parent ego state or their Child ego state and do not use their Adult, they are not in touch with the here and now.

If people exclude their Parent and Child, using only their Adult, they may be boring or robot-like without passion or compassion.

The Parent,
excluding the
Adult and Child

The Adult,
excluding the
Parent and Child

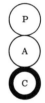

The Child,
excluding the
Parent and Adult

Rigidly responding from only one ego state is a serious enough personality problem to profit from professional help. However, many people favor one ego state over the other. This is the less serious ego boundary problem of being Constant Parent, Constant Adult, or Constant Child.

SOME PEOPLE USE THEIR PARENT EGO STATE CONSTANTLY

A person who operates primarily from the Parent ego state
often treats others, even business associates, as if they were
children. Such behavior can be found in a secretary who
"takes care of" everyone's problems at the office or in a
corporation boss who tries to run the personal lives of the
staff, who cannot be approached reasonably, or who displays
little or no sense of humor. Either knowingly or unknowingly
Constant Parents collect people who are willing to be
dependent upon or subordinate to them.

One type of Constant Parent is hardworking, has a strong
sense of duty, and often seeks positions of power. Making
judgments, being critical of others, and expressing moral
opinions are typical. Another type of Constant Parent is the
perpetual nurturer or rescuer who may play the role of
benevolent dictator, or may "come on" as a saintly person
who devotes a lifetime to helping others. This person is
the continual nurturer who is often drawn to one of the
"helping" professions and may be very effective. Yet, over-
indulging in caretaking keeps others unnecessarily dependent
and may do more harm than good.

EXERCISE 1. CONSTANT PARENT AND OCCUPATIONAL CHOICES

In your groups discuss and list the kinds of occupations that
the authoritarian type of Constant Parent might seek.

_____   _____

_____   _____

_____   _____

In your groups discuss and list the kinds of occupations that
the nurturing type of Constant Parent might seek.

_____   _____

_____   _____

_____   _____

SOME PEOPLE USE THEIR ADULT EGO STATE CONSTANTLY

The person who operates primarily as Constant Adult is consistently objective, uninvolved, and concerned primarily with facts and data processing. The appearance of being unfeeling or unsympathetic may result. This person may be a bore at a party and may be unable to show sympathy to someone who has a headache.

People who exhibit the rigid boundary problem of the Constant Adult may seek jobs that are object-oriented rather than people-oriented. They may select vocations where abstract thinking devoid of emotion is valued.

The Constant Adult often experiences trouble on a job if he or she is given a position that requires supervising others. With little caring Parent or fun-loving Child, relationships are likely to be sterile. Subordinates may be unhappy because so little stroking may be given. Many work situations suffer if there is no one acting as a nurturing Parent and no one to "joke around" like a Child.

EXERCISE 2.   CONSTANT ADULT AND OCCUPATIONAL CHOICES

In your groups discuss and list the kinds of occupations that people who constantly use their Adult might choose.

_____   _____

_____   _____

_____   _____

SOME PEOPLE USE THEIR CHILD EGO STATE CONSTANTLY

The person who operates primarily as Constant Child is
the one who is the perpetual little boy or girl who, like
Peter Pan, doesn't want to grow up. In this state thinking
independently, making personal decisions, or taking responsibility for actions are ignored. A man or woman who wants
to be "kept," babied, punished, rewarded, or applauded is
likely to seek out a Constant Parent who can afford to give
this type of care.
   People with this ego boundary problem are often successful
as performers on the stage or on the playing field. However,
without adequate Adult functioning, the performer may spend
his or her large salary impulsively, often ending up broke.

EXERCISE 3.   CONSTANT CHILD AND OCCUPATIONAL CHOICES

In your groups discuss and list the kinds of occupations that
people who constantly use their Child might seek.

_____	_____
_____	_____
_____	_____
_____	_____

EXERCISE 4.   YOUR EGO STATE PORTRAIT

Using circles of different sizes, draw your ego state portrait as you perceive
yourself most of the time. Your portrait might look something like the figures below.

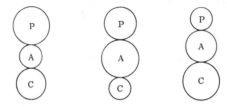

- Do you see yourself as having a favorite ego state?

- Does your portrait change when the situation changes? At work? At
  home? At school? At a party? Where else?

- Does it change with certain people? A boss? Subordinate? Spouse?
  Children? Friends? Who else?

- Now ask a child, spouse, friend, relative, and/or business associate to
  draw how he perceives you. Notice any differences?

After you have drawn your ego state portraits, both from your own perspective and that of others, ask yourself,

- Does this satisfy me? If not, what needs to be changed?

- What decisions do I need to make? What data do I need to gather?

EXERCISE 5.   YOUR EGOGRAM

Some people use one ego state more than the others. Draw an egogram [2]
of yourself estimating your use of ego state functions on a percentage basis
adding up to 100%.

 For example, on the job or in the classroom might look like:

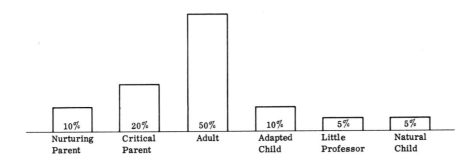

| 10%
Nurturing
Parent | 20%
Critical
Parent | 50%
Adult | 10%
Adapted
Child | 5%
Little
Professor | 5%
Natural
Child |

At home it may be more like:

Here and on the next page, draw your egogram for at least two situations.

Individual Egograms

_____

_____

Note to leader: If the situation warrants, have members of small
groups make egograms for each other and discuss them with each other.

ADULT THINKING CAN BE CONTAMINATED

The clear thinking of the Adult is often spoiled by contamination. When this occurs, rational problem solving is blocked.
Contamination can be thought of as an intrusion of the Parent
ego state and/or the Child ego state into the boundary of the
Adult ego state. Contamination occurs when the Adult accepts
as true some unfounded Parent beliefs or Child distortions,
and rationalizes and justifies these attitudes.

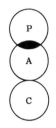

The Adult,
contaminated
by the Parent

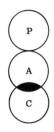

The Adult,
contaminated
by the Child

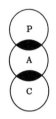

The Adult,
contaminated by the
Parent and Child

   In extreme cases, contamination from the Parent is
experienced as hallucinations which are sensory perception
of things that are not real. [3]   Hallucinations occur when
something not there is seen or voices that give commands or
make accusations are imagined.
   To a lesser degree, Parent contaminations are prejudices —
tenaciously held opinions which have not been examined on
the basis of objective data. Parental figures often express
their prejudices to children with such conviction that they
appear to be facts. The person who believes these Parental
opinions without evaluating them has a contaminated Adult.
   Severe contamination from the Child ego state often occurs
because of some delusion. A common one is the delusion of
grandeur. A belief that one is the savior or the ruler of
the world may result. Another common delusion is of being
persecuted. A person may erroneously believe he or she is
being poisoned, spied upon, or plotted against.
   In its less severe forms a person whose Child contaminates
his Adult has distorted perceptions of reality — illusions.
He may, for example, feel as if no one likes him and may
have no objective data as to whether or not it is true. Yet
he may believe that his feelings are the equivalent of
scientific facts.

EXERCISE 6. SEXUAL PREJUDICES

Work in small groups and complete the following with a list of at least 10
descriptive adjectives and/or phrases. Use only adjectives and/or phrases
that are common stereotypes.

Women are

_____   _____

_____   _____

_____   _____

_____   _____

_____   _____

_____   _____

_____   _____

Now do the same with:

Men are

_____   _____

_____   _____

_____   _____

_____   _____

_____   _____

_____   _____

_____   _____

Now discuss how such beliefs can affect life goals, choice of spouse, unrealistic expectations of self and others, and patterns of communication on
the job.

EXERCISE 7.   MASS MEDIA AND CONTAMINATION

Collect a packet of 5 different magazines. Look through them. Observe the images of men that are being promoted. Observe those images related to women.

Do the advertisements use women as sex objects? as continually loving mothers? as harried housewives? as what?

_____

_____

_____

_____

Do the advertisements use men as sex objects? as tough outdoors men? as overworked executives? as what?

_____

_____

_____

_____

Look for the ways in which the mass media tries to appeal to you. Which ego state gets hooked most frequently?

_____

_____

_____

_____

EXERCISE 8. ADJECTIVES TELL A STORY

Write the names of three people you dislike or avoid.
Without censoring your thoughts, make a list of five descriptive words that come to mind when you think of each
person.

_____	_____	_____
_____	_____	_____
_____	_____	_____
_____	_____	_____
_____	_____	_____

Now compare these lists. Is there any similarity of adjectives? For example, do you tend to classify or stereotype
people?

Do the people you've selected seem similar to one another?

Do your words reflect a prejudice against people of a certain
age? race? sex?

THINKING CAN BE CLARIFIED

Some problems have an emotional element. This usually
means that Parent ego state programming and/or Child ego
state programming is involved. For example, a person may be
Parent programmed to "Work hard but don't enjoy yourself."
This overly inhibits the Natural Child and guilt is experienced
if something enjoyeable occurs. Sometimes people would like
to change jobs, change a behavior pattern, improve family
relationships, consider more education, etc., but feel they
don't dare. This faulty thinking can be changed.

EXERCISE 9. PROBLEM-SOLVING TECHNIQUE

If you have a problem that needs solving, activate your Adult by following specific steps. Some steps may not apply to all problems but at least consider them as you move through the process.

1. Define the problem and write it down (you may find that what you thought was the problem wasn't the basic one).

2. What are your Parent's opinions, information, and behavior concerning this problem.

   ● List what each of your Parent figures would say or do about it.

   ● Listen to your Parents speaking in your head. Write down their shoulds, oughts, etc. Now list what they avoided and their non-verbal messages.

3. Next consider your Child's feelings, attitudes, and information about the problem.

   ● List the feelings you have that are related to the problem. Are these stamps or legitimate feelings?

   ● Are any games being played in connection with the problem?

   ● Does the problem fit into your constructive, destructive, or non-productive script? Are any manipulative roles being played?

4. Evaluate the above Parent and Child data with your Adult.

   ● What Parent attitudes hinder you in solving the problem? What Parent attitudes aid you in solving the problem?

   ● What Child feelings and adaptations hinder you in solving the problem? What Child feelings and adaptations aid you in solving the problem?

   ● What solution would please your Parent? Would it be appropriate or destructive for you to do this?

   ● What solution would please your Child? Would it be appropriate or destructive?

5. Imagine alternative ways to solve the problem. Do not censor any ideas. Instead, use your Little Professor and "brainstorm." Come up with as many possibilities as you can—even if some seem ridiculous.

6. Then consider internal and external resources necessary for each brainstorming solution. Are the resources available? Are they appropriate?

7. Estimate the probabilities of success from each alternative. Weed out those that are not possible.

8. Select two or three that are the most possible. On the basis of the facts and your creative imagination make your decision.

9. Be aware of the effects of your decision.

    Decisions that make you "feel good" may be satisfying to all ego states. A decision that makes you feel uncomfortable may have your Parent and/or Child fighting against it, may actually be harmful to yourself or others, or may be simply the wrong decision.

10. Establish the contract you need to carry out the decision. Raise the appropriate Adult questions that fit your contract.

11. Implement your decisions with action. If possible, test it first in a small way. Then move ahead with more power.

12. Evaluate the strengths and weaknesses of your plan as you go along. Make any necessary adjustments.

EXERCISE 10. PERSONALITY FACTORS IN PROBLEM SOLVING

Define a problem and then list the major factors that center around the problem you want to solve or the decision you want to make.

_____

_____

_____

_____

_____

_____

_____

_____

_____

_____

_____

_____

_____

_____

_____

_____

_____

Parent

Adult

Child

Now go back over each factor and decide which ego state that particular factor is most relevant to. If it is about the same for two ego states or more, draw lines to all. Draw a line from each factor to each ego state. After you have completed this task, consider the following questions.

Is only one ego state predominant in your consideration of this problem?

_____

_____

_____

Is this appropriate?

_____

Are all your ego states involved in this problem?

_____

Are you going against any particular ego state? _____

If so, which one? _____

How much is your Adult involved in solving this problem? In what ways? Is this an appropriate amount?

_____

_____

_____

_____

How much is your Child involved in this problem? In what ways? Is this an appropriate amount?

_____

_____

_____

_____

How much is your Parent involved in this problem? In what ways? Is this an appropriate amount?

_____

_____

_____

_____

Is the Parent involved in a constructive or destructive way?

_____

_____

Is there a solution that would "please" all three ego states?

_____

_____

If not, is there a solution that would please the Adult and

the Child?_____

_____

   Now select the most constructive factors on your list that
are the most important to your life goals. Make your
decision on the basis of satisfying all three ego states to
the extent that this is constructive. Become aware of any way
or tendency you have to "please" an ego state that may be
destructive to you.

_____

SUMMARY

The spontaneous use of personality resources can be affected
by ego boundary problems. If these ego boundaries are too
rigid, the psychic energy of a person is "locked" in one ego
state, excluding the others. This problem manifests itself
by a continuous use of one ego state — the person chooses to
act almost exclusively from the Parent, the Adult, or the
Child. The Adult's clear perception of current reality can
also be contaminated by prejudiced beliefs and childhood
delusions.
   For the Adult to gain executive control so that the person
can solve these problems, this ego state must be activated
and used. Everyone has this potential, even though for some
people it may not seem so. Berne makes the analogy that a
person may have a good radio, but it needs to be turned on
and tuned in before it can be heard clearly. [4] When your
Adult ego state is turned on and tuned in, it can help you
set the course of your life much more intelligently.

UNIT 7. THE WAYS PEOPLE STRUCTURE TIME BETWEEN BIRTH AND DEATH

Do you know someone who spends much of his time alone, withdrawn from other people?

Do you know someone who typically engages in a stereotyped, predetermined pattern of behavior that may have generations of tradition behind it?

Do you know people who pass much of their time talking about the weather or people who frequently send ulterior messages to others?

Do you know people who work as a team and get a job done or people who take time to experience an intimate moment of tenderness and authenticity?

If so, you have observed the various ways people structure their time between birth and death.

Being bored for a long time hastens emotional and physical deterioration in much the same way as inadequate stroking does. To avoid the pain of boredom, people seek something to do with their time. What parent has not heard a bored child whining, "Mama, what can I do now?" What married couple hasn't sat around musing, "What can we do this weekend?" What worker hasn't heard another one say, "I hate this job when there's not enough to do."

TIME IS STRUCTURED SIX WAYS

People structure their time in six possible ways. Sometimes they withdraw from other people; sometimes they engage in rituals or pastimes; sometimes they play psychological games; sometimes they work together; and occasionally they experience a moment of intimacy.

Withdrawal from others can be physical or psychological. This behavior can come from any of the three ego states. For example, if withdrawal comes from the Adapted Child it is often a replay of a person's childhood. Choosing withdrawal may have been a form of protection from pain or conflict or it may have been the result of training. A child told repeatedly "Go to your room and shut the door and don't come out until you have a smile on your face" can learn to withdraw behind a forced smile.

When a person withdraws psychologically, it is often into a fantasy world. Fantasies are likely to be of uncensored pleasure or violence, creative imaginings, or learned fears and catastrophic expectations. Everyone withdraws into fantasy from time to time. Who hasn't imagined all those great things that "could have been" said? Who hasn't engaged in some fanciful, uncensored pleasure? When listening to a dull speech, withdrawal into fantasy may be the best use of time.

Ritual transactions are simple and stereotyped complimentary transactions like everyday hellos and goodbyes. If someone says, "Good Morning, how are you?" the inquiry, in most instances, is not into the other person's health and feelings; what is expected is a ritualistic response, "Fine, how are you?" In this brief encounter both persons get maintenance strokes.

   Pastime transactions are those in which people pass time
with one another by talking about innocuous subjects, such
as the weather. These superficial exchanges are often used
between people who don't know each other well. For example,
at a dinner party it is not uncommon for people to pass the
time talking about occupations, cars, sports, the stock mar-
ket, recipes, children, decorating, and other neutral subjects.
   Games have certain advantages. One "advantage" of playing psychological games is to structure time. For example,
a secretary may play Blemish with the boss by taking only
a few minutes to point out that an "s" was forgotten on the
third person singular verb or that "absence" was misspelled.
   Other games, such as Debtor, can structure a lifetime.
For example, when a young married couple play Debtor, they
go into heavy debt for furniture, appliances, cars, boats,
and so on, and with each salary raise they go further into
debt — a bigger house, two cars, and so forth. For a whole
lifetime, no matter what they earn, they're always in debt.
When Debtor players play a "harder" game, they may end up
filing for bankruptcy or going to jail which fills even
more time.

Activities are ways of structuring time that deal with external reality and are commonly thought of as work, getting something done. Activities are often what people want to do, need to do, or have to do, such as preparing a memo, building a bridge, sewing a dress, programming a computer. In the midst of getting a job done, rituals, pastimes, games, and even intimacy may occur.

Intimacy involves genuine caring and authenticity. It occurs in moments that are free of games and free of exploitation—those rare moments of human contact that arouse feelings of tenderness, empathy, and affection.

The sense of intimacy can occur in the midst of a crowd or in a continuing friendship, in a marriage relationship, or at work. For example, a father looks into the tear-soiled face of his son who has just buried his dog. He puts his arm around the boy and says, "It's tough to bury a good friend." The boy melts into his father's arms, releasing his grief. For that moment they are intimate. Two people working together have an important proposal rejected. Without words, a feeling of understanding of their mutual disappointment passes between them. A man and woman open and trusting toward each other spontaneously embrace with warm affection.

Intimacy is sometimes frightening. It involves risk. It involves being vulnerable. Many times it seems easier to pass time or to play games than to risk feelings either of affection or of rejection.

EXERCISE 1. UNDERSTANDING WAYS PEOPLE USE THEIR TIME

In your group discuss and list at least three examples of the various ways time is structured in your organization, family, classroom, or whatever group is important to you.

Withdrawal

_____

_____

_____

Rituals

_____

_____

_____

Pastimes

_____

_____

_____

Activities

_____

_____

_____

Games

_____

_____

_____

Intimacy

_____

_____

_____

EXERCISE 2.   RECOGNIZING YOUR TIME-STRUCTURING PATTERNS

Recall how you structured your time over the last week.   Rank the various
ways of structuring your time as you were most involved (i.e., (1) rituals,
(2) activities).

_____

_____

_____

_____

_____

_____

Is the way you are structuring your time between birth and death the way you
really want it to be?

_____

If not, what do you want to change?

_____

_____

_____

EVERYONE CAN INCREASE AUTONOMY

A better opportunity to direct and take charge of one's own life is a major goal of transactional analysis. By understanding the influences that shape personality and the compulsions people live out according to a subconscious life script, and by being aware of the transactions that sometimes seem constructive or destructive, they can recognize the power they have over their own life goals. Those who accept responsibility for being the executives of their own lives can experience authenticity with the release or recovery of awareness, spontaneity, and intimacy.

People who become aware know themselves, their own past history but are not driven to repeat it. They have the freedom to feel and experience the hear and now. Their bodies, minds, and emotions work in unison.

Spontaneous people have options. They are free to choose behavior from all ego states. They can select from their past programming and discard what is destructive. They are able to continually grow and change with the situation.

People who are capable of intimacy can be open and authentic with themselves and others. They are able to be tender, caring, and affectionate and are able to accept the same from others.

EXERCISE 3.   ANALYZING YOUR AUTONOMY

Consider your own capacities for awareness, spontaneity, and intimacy. On a scale from 1 to 10, low to high, where do you see yourself now in relationship to:

Awareness

1 _____ 10

Spontaneity

1 _____ 10

Intimacy

1 _____ 10

Are you going to change any of these in the future?

_____

_____

PEOPLE CAN MAKE CONTRACTS FOR CHANGE

Making an Adult contract is a most important TA tool for strengthening the Adult. A contract is an Adult commitment to one's self and/or to someone else to make a change. Contracts can be established to change feelings, behavior, or psychosomatic problems.

A contract must be clear, concise, and direct. It involves (1) an awareness of a problem, (2) a decision to do something about the specific problem, (3) a statement of a clear goal in language simple enough for the inner Child to understand, and (4) the possibility of the goal's being fulfilled.

It is important that a contract be made by the Adult ego state. The Parent ego state may make a promise to put off a Child, and the Child ego state may make a "New Year's resolution" with no honest intention of keeping it. The Adult plays it straight!

EXERCISE 4. MAKING A CONTRACT

After having worked through this workbook, have you discovered any behavior pattern or attitude that you wish to change?

If so, make a contract with yourself, stating what you are going to change.

Now list three concrete steps you can take to fulfill your contract.

_____

_____

_____

Set a date for each of the steps.

_____

_____

_____

Set another date for the completion of your contract.

_____

P.S. from the authors

We believe that time is precious, that the use of time between birth and
death is important, and that the quality of living is primary. We believe
that when the curtain falls on our life we would like to say, "Good Show."

   We also believe people do not have to be enslaved by their past experiences. They can transcend past influences and respond with freedom in
the present. Using the Adult ego state, a person can re-decide what is
right and what is wrong based on actions that, when examined in their
reality, preserve the health and dignity of the person and of the human race.

FOOTNOTES AND REFERENCES

UNIT 1. THE SCRIPTS PEOPLE LIVE BY

1. Cf. Stephen B. Karpman, "Fairy Tales and Script Drama Analysis," Transactional Analysis Bulletin, 7, No. 26 (April 1968): 39–43.

2. Muriel James and Dorothy Jongeward, Born to Win: Transactional Analysis with Gestalt Experiments (Reading, Massachusetts: Addison-Wesley, 1971). See Chapter 1.

3. Eric Berne, Principles of Group Treatment (New York: Oxford University Press, 1964), pp. 269-278.

4. Eric Berne, Sex in Human Loving (New York: Simon & Schuster, 1971), p. 193.

5. Eric Berne, "Standard Nomenclature, Transactional Nomenclature," Transactional Analysis Bulletin, 8, No. 32 (October 1969): 112.

    Cf. Zelig Selinger, "The Parental Second Position in Treatment," Transactional Analysis Bulletin, 6, No. 21 (January 1967): 29.

UNIT 2. THE PERSONALITIES PEOPLE DEVELOP

1. Berne, Principles of Group Treatment, p. 364.

2. Eric Berne, Transactional Analysis in Psychotherapy (New York: Grove Press, 1961), p. 32.

3. Source Unknown.

4. Eric Berne, What Do You Do After You Say Hello? (New York: Grove Press, 1972), p. 272.

UNIT 4. STROKES AND THE PSYCHOLOGICAL TRADING STAMPS PEOPLE COLLECT

1. Eric Berne, Games People Play (New York: Grove Press, 1964), p. 15.

2.   Eric Berne, The Structure and Dynamics of Organizations and Groups (Philadelphia: J. B. Lippincott, 1963), p. 157.

3.   Berne, Principles of Group Treatment, pp. 286–288.

UNIT 5.   THE GAMES PEOPLE PLAY

1.   Cf. Stephen B. Karpman, "Fairy Tales and Script Drama Analysis," pp. 39–43.

UNIT 6.   THE BLOCKS TO PROBLEM SOLVING

1.   Berne, Transactional Analysis in Psychotherapy, pp. 39–40.

2.   John Dusay, "Egograms and the Constancy Hypothesis," Transactional Analysis Journal, 2, No. 3 (July 1972): 37.

3.   Berne, Transactional Analysis in Psychotherapy, p. 62.

4.   Berne, Principles of Group Treatment, p. 311.

UNIT 7.   THE WAYS PEOPLE STRUCTURE TIME BETWEEN BIRTH AND DEATH

1.   Berne, Games People Play, p. 178.

APPENDIX A

We have provided more exercises than most leaders have time to use. Nothing takes the place of the leader's good judgment as to the needs of the group with which he is working.

Since transactional analysis is both a tool for therapy and a tool for better communications in a nonclinical sense, we caution group leaders who are not trained clinicians not to act as therapists. For the application of transactional analysis to special fields, i.e., management, consulting, teacher's training, the basic concepts of transactional analysis are used to foster better self-understanding and better interpersonal relationships—particularly in the organizational setting.

Following are some suggestions for programs of different lengths:

One-day program

Cover the concepts in Units 2, 3, and 4, and (if pertinent to your group) 5.

Unit 2, The Personalities People Develop
Unit 3, The Transactions People Use
Unit 4, Strokes and the Psychological Trading Stamps People Collect
Unit 5, The Games People Play

Select only those exercises that reinforce what you want to reinforce and that there is time for. More can be covered in sessions if participants are assigned reading ahead. If possible, tell the participants ahead of time what parts are to be covered. This helps to avoid the feeling of incompleteness that occurs when something is only partially done. If your one day is followed by a half or full day later, parts of Units 1, 6, or 7 may be used.

Unit 1, The Scripts People Live By
Unit 6, The Blocks to Problem Solving.
Unit 7, The Ways People Structure Time Between Birth and Death

Two-day program

A similar plan to the one above may be used allowing, however, more time for the exercises and completing more of the exercises. You may choose to use parts from each unit, selecting those that fit your organization.

Thirty-hour program

For this long a session, we suggest that the Workbook be used in conjunction with Born to Win: Transactional Analysis with Gestalt Experiments (Reading, Massachusetts: Addison-Wesley, 1971). This gives the participants more in-depth information about transactional analysis, yet, with the exercises in the workbook designed for group learning, allows participants to work with one another.* However, the workbook can stand alone if an introductory overview of transactional analysis concepts is the goal of the sessions.

_____

* The experiments and exercises in <u>Born to Win</u> are designed primarily for individual learning.

APPENDIX B

The following bibliography is given for the person who wishes to be aware of other books and materials about Transactional Analysis. Most of these items can be ordered through

International Transactional Analysis Association
1772 Vallejo Street
San Francisco, California 94123

This association also publishes a Directory of Affiliates and Geographical List of Members and has available other publications not mentioned below.

BIBLIOGRAPHY

Eric Berne, Games People Play (New York: Grove Press, 1964).

Eric Berne, Layman's Guide to Psychiatry and Psychoanalysis (New York: Simon & Schuster, 1957).

Eric Berne, Principles of Group Treatment (New York: Oxford University Press, 1964).

Eric Berne, Sex in Human Loving (New York: Simon & Schuster, 1971).

Eric Berne, The Structure and Dynamics of Organizations and Groups (Philadelphia: J.B. Lippincott, 1963).

Eric Berne, Transactional Analysis is Psychotherapy (New York: Grove Press, 1961).

Eric Berne, What Do You Say After You Say Hello? (New York: Grove Press, 1972).

Thomas Harris, I'm OK-You're OK: A Practical Guide to Transactional Analysis (New York: Harper & Row, 1969).

Muriel James, cassette recording, "The OK Boss," professionally narrated (Success Motivation Institute, Waco, Texas).

Muriel James, cassette recording, "Changing Yourself through Transactional Analysis," an interview with Muriel James, produced by Psychology Today (New York: Ziff David Publishing Company).

Muriel James, Breaking Free: Self-Reparenting for a New Life (Reading, Massachusetts: Addison-Wesley, 1981).

Muriel James, Marriage is for Loving (Reading, Massachusetts; Addison-Wesley, 1979).

Muriel James, Transactional Analysis for Moms and Dads (Reading: Massachusetts: Addison-Wesley, 1974).

Muriel James and Dorothy Jongeward, Born to Win: Transactional Analysis with Gestalt Experiments (Reading: Massachusetts: Addison-Wesley, 1971).

Muriel James and Dorothy Jongeward, The People Book: Transactional Analysis for Students (Menlo Park, California: Addison-Wesley, 1975).

Muriel James and Louis Savary, A New Self (Reading, Massachusetts: Addison-Wesley, 1977).

Dorothy Jongeward and Dru Scott, Affirmative Action for Women: A Practical Guide for Women and Management (Dorothy Jongeward Associates, Inc., 724 Ironbark Court, Orinda, California 94563; revised, 1975).

Dorothy Jongeward and Philip Seyer, Choosing Success: Human Relationships on the Job (New York: John Wiley Publishing Company, Inc., 1978).

Dorothy Jongeward and contributors, Everybody Wins: Transactional Analysis Applied to Organizations (Dorothy Jongeward Associates, Inc., revised 1976).

Dorothy Jongeward and Muriel James, Winning Ways in Health Care: Transactional Analysis for Effective Communication (Reading, Massachusetts: Addison-Wesley, 1981).

Dorothy Jongeward and Dru Scott, Women As Winners: A Guide to Growth, Understanding, and Authenticity (Reading, Massachusetts: Addison-Wesley, revised 1982).

Dorothy Jongeward, cassette recording, "An Overview of Transactional Analysis," professionally narrated (Dorothy Jongeward Associates, Inc.).

Dorothy Jongeward, "Personal Stress Management," a two-cassette binder narrated by Dr. Jongeward for deep relaxation and stress reduction (Dorothy Jongeward Associates, Inc., 1982).

Paul McCormick and Leonard Campos, Introduce Yourself to Transactional Analysis (Stockton, California: San Joaquin Transactional Analysis Study Group, 1969).

Claude M. Steiner, Games Alcoholics Play (New York: Grove Press, 1971).

Transactional Analysis Bulletin (back issues) now the Transactional Analysis Journal. (Write International Transactional Analysis Association, 1772 Vallejo Street, San Francisco, California 94123).

APPENDIX C. POSSIBLE EGO STATE RESPONSES

Analyzing Ego State Vocabulary and Body Language

PARENT

Sample words and phrases

should, don't, must, ought, always, never, now what, if I were you, let me help you, because I said so, don't ask questions, do not disturb, be good, what will the neighbors say, there there, sweetie, honey, and dearie.

You are: bad, good, stupid, ugly, beautiful, smart, ridiculous, naughty, evil, talented, cute, all wet, horrible, a trial, a blessing, a brat, an angel, absurd, asinine, shocking.

Try, don't be afraid; come on now; see, it doesn't hurt; don't worry; I'll take care of you; here's something to make you feel better.

Gestures and Postures

Pointing an accusing or threatening finger; a pat on the back; consoling touch; pounding on the table; rolling eyes upward in disgust; tapping feet or wringing hands in impatience; shaking head to imply "no-no" or "OK!" Arms folded across chest with chin set; face tilted up looking down nose; holding and/or rocking someone.

Tone of voice

Sneering, punitive, condescending, encouraging, supportive, sympathetic.

Facial expressions

Scowl; encouraging nod; furrowed brow; set jaw; angry; sympathetic or proud eyes; smile; frown; loving; hostile; disapproving.

ADULT

Sample words and phrases

How; when; who; what; where; why; probability; alternative; result; yes; no; what are the facts; this is not proven but opinion; check it out; what has been done to correct it so far; it's 4:30 P.M.; what are the reasons; have you tried this; mix two parts with one part; this is how it works; let's take it apart and look at it; let's look for the causes; according to the statistics...; change is indicated; the meeting is at 2:00 P.M. Friday.

Gestures and Postures

Straight (not stiff) posture; eye contact that's level; pointing something out (i.e., direction) with finger; listening by giving feedback and checking out understanding; interested.

Tone of voice

Clear without undue emotion; calm; straight; confident; inquiring and giving information.

Facial expression

Thoughtful; watching attentively; quizzical; lively; here and now responsiveness; eyes alert, confident.

CHILD

Sample words and phrases

Gosh, wow; gee whiz; can't; won't; gimme; dunno; want; wish; (any kind of baby talk); mine; eek.   Ain't I cute; look at me now; did I do all right; I'm scared; help me; do it for me; nobody loves me; you make me cry; it's your fault; I didn't do it; he's no good; mine is better than yours; I'm going to tell on you; you'll be sorry; I wanta go home; let's play; phooey on this old job; more candy; I hope everybody loves me.

Gestures and Postures

Slumped; dejected; temper tantrums; batting eyelashes; joyful or exhilerated posture; curling up; skipping; squirming; nose thumbing; (other obscene gestures); nail biting; raising hand to speak.

Tone of voice

Giggling; gurgling; whining; manipulating; sweet talk; asking permission; swearing; spitefulness; teasing; sullen silence; taunting; needling; belly laughing; excitement; talking fast and loud; playfulness.

Facial expression

Teary eyed; pouting; eyes looking upward at another; downcast eyes; joyfulness; excited; curious; psyching things out; tilted head; flirty; looking innocent and wide-eyed; woe-be-gone; helplessness; admiration.